"This book is a must-read for any nonprofit organization that wants to have a voice in the marketplace of ideas where social policy is formed, debated, and promoted. I have worked on social justice campaigns with CCMC many times over the past 20 years, and I know from experience that the advice in this book works."

—Wade Henderson, president and CEO, Leadership Conference on Civil Rights

"In the 21st century world in which we live, media dominates our lives and keeps us connected to everything that is going on, globally and locally. This book, and its authors, provides the tools to master the strategies, skills, and techniques of communications. Any nonprofit organization striving for social change must see it as one of *the* most important guidebooks in their tool kit of references and how-to tips for their communications work."

—Donna Hall, president and CEO, Women Donors Network

"To make social change in this world it is imperative that nonprofit organizations think through how to tell their stories. Communication is a critical element in any strategic vision of change and the Communications Consortium Media Center knows how to do it. They are experienced, strategic, and thoughtful. This book is element number one in building a communication plan for change."

—Susan King, vice president, external affairs, and director, journalism initiative, special initiatives and strategy, Carnegie Corporation of New York

"To have an impact in the global world of the 21st century, one must master the techniques of communications. Keep this book handy and it will help you become more effective and more confident in your dealings with the news media— whether you're taking on your first communications campaign or your fiftieth."

—Safiye Cagar, director of information and external relations division, United Nations Population Fund

Strategic Communications for Nonprofits

A Step-by-Step Guide to
Working with the Media

Second Edition

Kathy Bonk, Emily Tynes, Henry Griggs, and Phil Sparks

A publication of the Communications Consortium Media Center

Foreword by Larry Kirkman

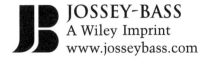

JOSSEY-BASS
A Wiley Imprint
www.josseybass.com

Published by Jossey-Bass
A Wiley Imprint
989 Market Street, San Francisco, CA 94103-1741—www.josseybass.com

Jossey-Bass books and products are available through most bookstores. To contact Jossey-Bass directly call our Customer Care Department within the U.S. at 800-956-7739, outside the U.S. at 317-572-3986, or fax 317-572-4002.

Jossey-Bass also publishes its books in a variety of electronic formats. Some content that appears in print may not be available in electronic books.

Library of Congress Cataloging-in-Publication Data

Strategic communications for nonprofits: a step-by-step guide to working with the media/Kathy Bonk . . . [et al.]; foreword by Larry Kirkman. —2nd ed.

    p. cm. — (The Jossey-Bass nonprofit guidebook series)

Rev. ed. of: Jossey-Bass guide to strategic communications for nonprofits/ Kathy Bonk, Henry Griggs, Emily Tynes. c1999.

    Includes index.

    ISBN 978-0-470-18154-6 (pbk.)

    1. Nonprofit organizations—Management. 2. Corporations—Public relations. I. Bonk, Kathy. II. Jossey-Bass guide to strategic communications for nonprofits.

    HD62.6.B66 2008

    658.8'02—dc22
                                        2008027253

Printed in the United States of America

SECOND EDITION

PB Printing   10 9 8 7 6 5 4 3 2 1

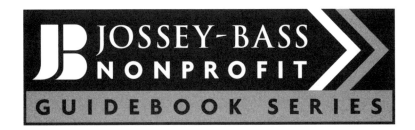

The Jossey-Bass Nonprofit Guidebook Series

The Jossey-Bass Nonprofit Guidebook Series provides new to experienced nonprofit professionals and volunteers with the essential tools and practical knowledge they need to make a difference in the world. From hands-on workbooks to step-by-step guides on developing a critical skill or learning how to perform an important task or process, our accomplished expert authors provide readers with the information required to be effective in achieving goals, mission, and impact.

Contents

For Dick Boone and in memory of Lisa Goldberg.
Thank you for your gifts of wisdom, patience,
and unwavering support.

Foreword

Larry Kirkman, Dean, School of Communication, American University

IN THIS GUIDE, the Communications Consortium Media Center (CCMC) provides the compass points and tools that nonprofits need to strengthen their organizations and become innovative agents of social change—to engage, inform, and persuade their targeted public audiences and to recruit, involve, motivate, and equip their activist constituencies. CCMC's knowledge is drawn from twenty years of experience advising organizations on their media operations and helping them conduct public education and issue advocacy campaigns. Since 1988, under the sustained leadership of Kathy Bonk, Phil Sparks, and Emily Tynes, CCMC has worked collaboratively with hundreds of nonprofits and scores of coalitions, creating a laboratory of professional practice that has explored the full range of strategic options and tested the payoffs for organizations and the causes they pursue. Their collective intelligence is distilled into best practices, vivid case studies, and proven methods for planning and evaluation. It's more than a menu of techniques—it's about how and when to use them, how to play them off one another, how to combine them into a comprehensive media plan. It's about the integration of sophisticated message research, strategic media relations, powerful media products, targeted advertising, and online communications.

There are wide gaps at the intersection of media, technology, and democracy that nonprofits can fill—in policy debates, issue advocacy, and public education. When politicians fail to address the issues that matter, when news companies cut back on investigative reporting, when media barrage the public with fearsome and unintelligible images of catastrophe, making their audiences feel helpless and hopeless, nonprofits can provide the evidence and testimony that drive public engagement and promote solutions to social problems. They can speak up and talk back to the powers that be—whether defending human rights abroad and civil liberties at home, closing the gap between economic haves and have-nots, framing global warming, or denying a call to war.

The very first edition of this book, *Strategic Media,* was published in 1992 by the Benton Foundation as part of a package of nine media and technology guides, with the title *Strategic Communications for Nonprofits.* I was director of the foundation and coeditor, with Karen Menichelli, of the series. We were on a mission—calling on nonprofit leaders to adopt an integrated and comprehensive approach to media. In the fragmented and cluttered media marketplace, many nonprofit leaders felt overwhelmed and demoralized. This series was a spirited response to the cynics who saw the media as a problem—not a solution.

The Benton series asserted the necessity for coordinated and consistent investment in communications. Major private foundations, including Ford, MacArthur, Carnegie Corporation, and Robert Wood Johnson, bought into the cause and distributed the set of guides to thousands of their grantees.

In 1999, CCMC picked up the banner of the Benton series with the next edition of this book, reviving the title *Strategic Communications for Nonprofits.* And now in this edition, it has restated and refreshed their lessons.

It's not news that nonprofits need to rethink their communications strategies for an Internet generation that has abandoned newspapers and national television networks and is tapping into multiple sources of information on demand and using and producing blogs. The digital generation wants trusted sources *and* attitude. It wants to talk back. It wants to have an ongoing conversation that blurs the traditional roles of reader and reporter, professional and amateur, personal and political, volunteer and voter.

The onslaught of the digital age has put us all on a new footing. As the media environment buckles and shifts, as new forms of technology emerge and mutate, the business, ethical, and creative challenges in communications are formidable. How do we connect to audiences who feel there is too much to take in, too much to do anything about, when everyone can have a channel and the tools of production are cheap and relatively easy to use?

Nonprofit organizations have valuable assets to deploy in the digital environment—knowledge and content, trust and brand. They are becoming news and information providers, linking directly to their audiences, building social networks, and partnering with media companies.

There is no easy road map for the emergence of a vigorous and inclusive public culture, but we need to anticipate it and can help shape it by working across professional disciplines with media strategists, creative storytellers, and investigative journalists. Not doing so is a failure of nerve and imagination. And we have to ask the toughest questions about truth and transparency, credibility and conscience: Who has a voice? Who has access to the social, political, civil rights, and economic benefits of an information society? How do we adapt the standards and values of journalism to the creation of an enabling communications environment that we want to work and live in?

Nonprofits and their funders have a significant role to play. If we continue to get smart together, to reinvent our nonprofit organizations as communicating organizations, each of us, in our own way, can help determine the shape of things to come.

Acknowledgments

THIS BOOK IS the result of many heads, hands, and hearts. We deeply appreciate the dedication of numerous members of our terrific CCMC staff: Jason Shevrin, Laura Rogers, Royela Kim, Susan Boerstling, and Kristen Hagan; they arrived at the office early, stayed late, and worked weekends to proofread or format the manuscript. Our thanks also go to CCMC staff members Linda Zerden, Micheline Kennedy, Donna Morris, Jenny Williams, Val Franchel, and Emily Breton for their encouragement and motivation. The members of our board of directors have been our staunchest supporters, and we are grateful for their confidence in us and their enthusiasm for our work. We especially appreciate the support of our board chair, Ken Nochimson, and our executive committee, comprising Raydean Acevedo, who helped keep us going on the final deadline day, Dick Boone, Al Kramer, and Marlene Johnson. Board members Frank Smith, Juan Sepulveda, and Wouter Meijer have been guiding lights. And, in the memory of Mal Johnson, we thank her and other journalists who have taught us about the importance of keeping relationships fresh and professional.

CCMC has been blessed with the talents of many individuals whom we consider a part of our extended family. A special thank you is due to Carole Ashkinaze, who edited the first edition and was especially helpful in meeting our final deadline for this edition; Joanne Omang, who helped edit and proofread while adding important insights into the first edition of the book; and Andrea Camp, a confidant and creative partner.

Much of the information in the book is a distillation of the experiences and insights of individuals whom we also consider to be part of CCMC's network of colleagues. We are especially fortunate to have had the opportunity to work with the following people: Thoraya Obaid, Safiye Cagar, and the IERD team at UNFPA the UN Population Fund, including Sarah

Craven, our office mate and trusted colleague; Donna Hall, Wendy Wolf, Margery Loeb, Friederike Merke, and Kathy Barry at the Women Donors Network; Beth Shulman, our partner who has enlightened us on low-wage work and more; Douglas Gould, a talented strategist; and Kelly Burke, a media-readiness coach.

Trudi Baldwin, the director of the M.S. Program in Strategic Communications at Columbia University, provided invaluable insights on improving this version of the book. She offered advice on a revised outline that enhanced greatly the understanding of strategic communications. Reviewer Emily Whitfield also made helpful suggestions and ideas.

At the exact right moment, Jason Salzman, president of Cause Communications, coordinated the second True Spin Conference in Denver. (This is a must-attend for any organization wanting to learn strategic communications.) We thank him for being such a great supporter and collaborator. His contribution to the field of strategic communications is unsurpassed.

A significant portion of the discussion on message development and polling was gleaned from our associations with pollsters Vince Breglio, John Russonello, Nancy Belden, Celinda Lake, and Geof Garin. The chapter on responding to a crisis and managing backlash could not have been written without help from Mindy Good for the original guide and our colleagues at the Annie E. Casey Foundation for the opportunity to work with their grantees. They provided valuable written materials from which we were able to glean concepts and case studies.

We have had the opportunity to develop and test the practices described in the book in part due to our work funded by many philanthropic organizations, donors, partners, and nonprofits. We especially want to acknowledge some of the friends and funders who have enabled us to venture into new areas of learning or to move forward during critical moments of an initiative. For these opportunities, we say many, many thanks to Sono Aibe, Peggy Ayers, Tony Berkley, Laura and Dick Chasin, Alan and Suzanne Dworsky, Kathleen Feeley, Nicole Gray, Susan King, John Kowal, Tom Layton, Cathy Lerza, Lance Lindbloom, Geri Mannion, Wanda Mial, Anne Mosle, Helen Neubourne, Greg Taylor, Kathy Toner, and Alandra Washington.

Thanks also to Diana Meehan and Gary David Goldberg for making our first grant and believing in us for the past twenty years.

Throughout this book, we have quoted many individuals with whom we have worked. We wish to thank each of them for allowing us to share their experiences. Their contributions have enriched the book and the life of our organization.

The Benton Foundation, with support from Charles and Marjorie Benton, Larry Kirkman, and Karen Menichelli, provided resources for a very early edition of this manual, for which we are forever grateful.

The first edition of this book was made possible in part by the Charles H. Revson Foundation. Eli Evans and Lisa Goldberg have been true believers in our work over the past twenty years, and we have been privileged to learn from both of them. Just before Lisa died unexpectedly in January 2007, she insisted we start working on a revised edition. She provided new ideas, insights, and the motivation to start rewriting. The statements and views expressed, however, are solely our responsibility.

Finally, special thanks go to our spouses and partners, Marc, Jill, Ben, and Ann. Again, we missed important weekends and evenings with you, but it has been well worth the sacrifice.

About the Authors

Kathy Bonk established the Communications Consortium Media Center (CCMC) in 1988 and is its executive director. Over the past thirty years, she has been at the forefront of media campaigns that marked a sea change in domestic and global policies affecting women, children, and families with the support of major foundations and large donors. Prior to her work in the nonprofit sector, Kathy worked in government as a public information officer in the U.S. Department of State and in the Voting Section of the Civil Rights Division of the Department of Justice. She directed the Media Project for the NOW Legal Defense and Education Fund. She has a degree in communications from the University of Pittsburgh, and in 1988 was awarded a fellowship with the Kellogg Foundation's National Leadership Program.

• • •

Emily Tynes is a founder of CCMC who has been involved in the field of communications for three decades. She has worked as a journalist, a public relations executive, and an activist. Following the 9/11 terrorist attacks, a period of unprecedented assault on civil liberties, Emily became the communications director for the national office of the American Civil Liberties Union. Emily's work as a communications strategist encompassed a range of issues, including women's rights, racial equity, energy and the environment, and the health concerns of women of color. She has a degree in English from Howard University.

• • •

Henry Griggs is a writer and media relations consultant and a founder of CCMC. Henry worked with the Center on Budget and Policy Priorities in Washington DC for twelve years, four of them as communications director. The group is noted for its highly active media relations program, and was named one of the "most effective nonprofits founded in recent U.S. history." Henry was later communications director of Human Rights First in New York. A graduate of Harvard College, he worked in the election and survey unit of CBS News in New York, and conducted media events in thirty-five states for a national union of public employees.

• • •

Phil Sparks has twenty-five years of experience working in public interest communications. He specializes in family projects at CCMC. Phil was previously associate director for communications of the U.S. Census Bureau, director of public affairs for the American Federation of State, County and Municipal Employees (AFSCME); associate director of the President's Commission on Pension Policy; and chief of staff to former U.S. Representative Thomas J. Downey (NY). He is a founder of CCMC.

About CCMC: Communications Strategies for Policy Change

CCMC WAS FOUNDED in 1988 in response to the extraordinary, growing power of the media and of emerging communications technologies to shape public attitudes and public policy. The basis of our work is the principle that in a democratic society, informed dialogue is the cornerstone of good public policy. Our mission is to develop communications strategies for policy change.

From our offices in Washington DC, we have guided dozens of major communications initiatives that have influenced public debate in ways that respect and support individual rights, healthy families, cultural diversity, and a sustainable environment. We are proud to say that our work has helped refocus local, state, national, and global conversations about the future of communities, families, children, and youth, and about global health, population, and gender equality, with profound implications for policymaking. For example, a key tenet of our early work on the status of women around the world was our Women's Rights Are Human Rights campaign, which successfully redefined human rights to include an end to violence against women. A new idea at the time, this has informed every major international agreement since then, leading to measurable global improvements in schooling, health, self-sufficiency, and political influence for women and families.

CCMC works to mobilize public opinion through education campaigns with policy experts and organizations that share similar goals and concerns. Typically this is a collaborative process that involves dozens of prominent organizations working together for three to five years on specific communications objectives and goals. Our approach places heavy emphasis on research and cultivation of contacts at all levels in the United States and around the world.

A hallmark of our work has been our ability to weave the varied resources and often disparate perspectives of our partner organizations into integrated and collaborative strategies based on shared values.

As described in this book, often what holds these groups together is state-of-the-art public opinion research and analysis of trends in news of specific issues. From a shared base of knowledge, we work with our partners to shape resonant messages and to cultivate skilled and credible messengers. In this way, we have shown that even groups with limited resources can reach influential segments of the public and the news media, help bring neglected issues forward, and reframe public understanding in ways that lead to better policies.

Specific principles guide our work. First, the focus of each public education campaign is the issue or issues at hand, not the promotion of individuals or organizations. Second, collaboration among nonprofits that share policy goals is an effective and efficient way to gain credibility and influence among the media. And, finally, communications and outreach programs and the effective use of new communications technologies will enhance the goals of nonprofit organizations and provide opportunities and development.

Even the best plans need skillful implementation. Thus CCMC offers ongoing assistance to our partner groups in the day-to-day work of framing messages, preparing press materials, placing stories and op-eds, developing audio podcasts and video webcasts, coordinating media outreach activities, building press lists, and more. We provide training for spokespeople and communications staff, both beginners and seasoned pros, to help them become more confident in the use of these tools, and self-sufficient.

CCMC is a nonprofit 501(c)(3) organization with general support and special project funding from a wide range of individual donors and foundations. We are located in downtown Washington DC, within a few blocks of the National Press Club.

· · ·

CommunicationsConsortium **Media**Center
401 Ninth Street, NW, Suite 450
Washington, DC 20004
Telephone: 202-326-8700
Fax: 202-682-2154
E-mail: info@ccmc.org
www.ccmc.org

Introduction

THE EDITION OF this book published in 1999 was a nuts-and-bolts guide that addressed the specific needs of nonprofits, government agencies, traditional charities, and advocacy groups in designing and implementing successful communications strategies. Since then, those needs have only grown. The nonprofit sector has expanded in size and scope, while the challenges of a changing media environment in an age of global communications and declining news audiences have increased considerably.

This second edition builds on the earlier work and pays far more attention to what was then a nascent phenomenon: the Internet. But many of the principles and practices detailed in the first edition are still valid today. The book is intended primarily for groups targeting U.S. media, many with bureaus around the world, although key concepts, such as framing specific messages with widely shared values, are universal. And the principles work for all groups globally: no matter what their size or experience, nonprofits can use this guide to enhance their profiles in the media, increase name recognition, boost fundraising, recruit membership, and advance changes in public policy.

The advice in the book is based on the professional experience of four seasoned practitioners of communications in the nonprofit world. The early chapters explore the basic principles and elements of a strategic communications strategy, the essentials of research that will define the target audiences you need to reach, and how to develop the messages and messengers to reach them. This discussion of basic theory and practice is not intended as an academic exercise. Rather, it is an effort to give you a grounding in how to think for yourself in designing communications strategy, as no book can address every circumstance that might arise.

Later chapters address specific issues, such as earning good media coverage, building partnerships to increase available resources, and handling a crisis. Although it is possible to absorb useful information by referring to particular chapters of interest, you will probably find that the practical advice in the later chapters is more meaningful in the context of the earlier exploration of fundamentals.

With a clear mission and the right communications skills, even small volunteer organizations can succeed in designing, planning, and implementing strategic grassroots initiatives. And those organizations with greater resources will learn from case studies how a fully executed national strategy comes together. We hope this second version of our guidebook will help all nonprofits and anyone who endeavors to communicate in the public interest.

Chapter 1

The Basics of Strategic Communications

How can we get people talking about the real problems in our society?

What does it take to get coverage of important issues in newspapers and on the nightly news?

What is the best way to protect and expand our organization's communications budget?

People responsible for communications in nonprofit groups often find themselves asking questions like these, and more:

How can I build relationships with reporters?

What can be done about coverage of political campaigns that focuses on personalities instead of issues?

How can we get coverage of our group and issues that translates into more members and fundraising success?

One way to start answering these questions is to have a sound, well-planned communications strategy. Such a strategy goes far beyond the basics of public relations, which typically have included media lists, regular press releases, and occasional events. You also need to have an understanding of your target audiences, changes in the news industry, and how issues move through the media "food chain." New technologies, the Internet, and trends affecting journalism are dramatically changing the nature of media.

Strategic communications do include media outreach, but not as a stand-alone activity; rather, they must be integrated into other organizational functions, such as fundraising and membership building. Being strategic is not simply reacting to events, but anticipating and creating them. When successfully integrated into other management functions, strategic communications are tools for organizational leaders to use in both day-to-day operations and long-range planning for the growth and success of the entire operation.

Still, many nonprofit organizations operate as if e-mailing press releases and reaction statements, and holding press conferences now and then were sufficient ways to rally public support. They are not enough by themselves.

Good media coverage is a prized commodity, and it is built on a foundation of strong working relationships with key journalists and pursued through a well thought out plan of action. Such a plan typically includes carefully crafting messages, targeting reporters on a story-by-story basis, and receiving strategic guidance from polls and market research, which can be surprisingly affordable. Other important elements include building teams, framing messages, telling stories that will resonate with target audiences, training spokespeople, developing and marketing appropriate written materials, identifying opportunities to make news, and creating a system for evaluating progress.

A Built-in Advantage

Perhaps the first strategic insight for nonprofit communications is that there is a built-in advantage simply in being a nonprofit: what you are "pitching" to a reporter is meant to make a better world, not a bigger profit or an enhanced bottom line, and that approach often means a better story for journalists to cover. It is true that a group largely focused on advocacy in the state legislature or Congress may not be in quite the same position as, for example, a local homeless shelter or social service organization that is seen as purely charitable and does not engage in lobbying. But in most cases, nonprofits may have a foot in the door with journalists because of the special role nonprofits play in society.

Nonprofits may also be in a better position to provide personal stories and appeals to conscience and emotion than for-profit businesses. Finding good real-life stories in the ranks of your members, volunteers, or partners is important for a strategic communications plan, whether your work is strictly charitable, wholly directed at policy change, or someplace in between. For many audiences within the general public, and as a general trend in an age of information overload, personal stories are the ones that really matter. Reporters are always looking to "put a face" on their stories.

But as we outline in Chapter Four on developing messages, focusing too intently on a personal story or "portrait" can leave people with the sense that "it's their problem (and not mine)."

Lori Dorfman of the Berkeley Media Studies Group has compared so-called portrait and landscape stories in the media, observing that often change comes from the "fuller and broader perspective" on a situation.

Good Communications Affect Your Whole Organization

Many of the same stories and appeals that make for good media outreach have equal value in fundraising and membership recruitment activity. For instance, a group might place a newspaper article that focuses on one family as representative of a larger problem or trend. The article could then be posted on the group's Web site along with a short video interview with the people quoted in the newspaper. That link could also be sent to television reporters and producers, as evidence that the story passed muster with the newspaper and that the subject could do a good television interview. This might lead to a segment on the local television news, which could itself be posted on the Web site. Throughout this process, a savvy communications director is also e-mailing messages to potential members or donors to demonstrate your group's general impact and media smarts while asking for funds to expand media activities.

Working Collaboratively

Many nonprofits with a goal of changing public policy or raising awareness seek to enhance their clout by engaging in ongoing collaborative relationships or ongoing coalitions that strategize, advertise, and sometimes lobby together. Of course, for-profit businesses also collaborate and work in coalitions, but nonprofits are different in this respect too because they aren't driven by commercial competitiveness; they tend to collaborate with groups that complement their group's goals and culture.

With the rise of advocacy activities, strategists working with nonprofits have developed and refined a collaborative model for change-oriented groups that is centered on the development of a communications strategy, but goes far beyond simply planning media outreach. One element of the collaborative model is that groups must find common ground in the message they want to bring to the public, and the process of determining that message can itself build a working team. When partner organizations can weave their resources and perspectives into a collaborative strategy based on shared values, they benefit through better fundraising and constituent recruitment too.

Solid public opinion research and analysis of news trends on complex issues are keys to bringing and keeping such groups together. From a shared knowledge base, groups can work as partners to shape key messages and to cultivate skilled and credible messengers. Through such collaboration, groups with limited resources can influence the news media, help bring neglected issues forward, and reframe public understanding in ways that lead to better policies.

Building Media Skills

Another positive trend for nonprofits is that grantmakers and the foundation world have begun offering media training and skill building for their grantees. Major foundations, including the Carnegie Corporation of New York, the William and Flora Hewlett Foundation, and the W. K. Kellogg Foundation, are trendsetters in this arena. For example, in the Midwest, the Chicago-based Community Media Workshop, a nonprofit brainchild of journalists and media relations experts, is helping community groups connect with media to promote news that matters. This workshop has trained thousands of spokespeople and media strategists on evolving trends, offering practical tips for a modest cost. Others based on this model are springing up across the United States and around the world.

Academia is also responding to the demands for communications strategists. Columbia University in New York City has a master's degree program in strategic communications, and American University in Washington operates the Institute for Strategic Communication for Nonprofits, to name just two. Nearly all schools of communications have courses on strategic communications built on many of the strategies outlined in the following chapters. In addition, cognitive linguists in colleges and universities are providing important insights into how brain research combined with an understanding of language development can guide framing and messaging activities.

• • •

All these trends in journalism, philanthropy, academia, and technology can help identify and enhance channels of believable information, making the case for a larger investment and more sophisticated approach to strategic communications.

Organizational Values

The strategic communications programs that work best are firmly rooted in an organization's values and purpose. Your communications plan should support your organization's goals and mission statement. Communication is a tool, not an end in itself; neither a tail wagging the dog nor a quick fix for organizational challenges but, rather, one factor in your success.

Our work in the world of nonprofit communications has demonstrated time and again that public awareness of a nonprofit's activities and positions on issues is only one part of the picture. Good communications can also change attitudes both inside and outside an organization and enhance the prospects for success of almost any program or initiative you undertake. That's because a successful communications strategy ensures that ongoing activities are aligned to support the organization's long-term goals, its mission and values.

The funding community understands the importance of values-based messaging. For example, Alan Jenkins, a top executive from the Ford Foundation, founded the Opportunity Agenda based on the lessons from numerous grantees. His group now provides critical insights into the core American values around the concept of "opportunity," which encompasses fairness, equality, freedom, and civil liberties.

Such a strategic approach for nonprofits can lead to significant social change, increase an organization's membership, and move its financial bottom line well into the black, all at the same time. Conversely, nonprofits and public agencies that fail to understand the importance of building media strategies on the foundation of their mission and values make their overall work harder and less believable.

Even a small start-up organization can influence public opinion and public policy with a well-planned, well-executed communications strategy.

- Five years after its founding, the tiny but media-savvy International Campaign to Ban Land Mines won the 1997 Nobel Peace Prize.

- In 2007, a group called Numbers USA organized a populist revolt that derailed immigration legislation backed by the White House and top congressional leaders. Part of the group's strategy consisted of organizing the sending of one million faxes to Congress, but numbers don't tell the whole story. The messages contained in those faxes were successful in large part because they focused on policy questions and were scrubbed of all xenophobic language.

- A cover story in *Ms.* magazine, combined with the support of a handful of groups working to end sweatshop factory conditions in the Mariana Islands (a U.S. territory in the South Pacific), was able to turn around a decade of abuse by convincing Congress to apply U.S. labor standards and laws to employers there.

Why Nonprofits Resist Effective Communications Tools

Not every group will be able or willing, or will even have the need, to conduct a full-blown strategic communications plan. But preparing to operate in the new communications environment is a sound practice for every nonprofit organization. Many recognize this, but fail to use the tools of modern communications for a variety of reasons, which we discuss here.

Levels of Investment and Resources

Smaller organizations and agencies may not think that they can possibly compete with well-funded, established institutions, so they do not bother to try. Nonprofit groups and public agencies may hesitate to take on additional tasks if they are understaffed and overcommitted.

But with good communications work, small groups can make much more efficient use of their limited resources. Some succeed by pooling resources with other groups that share their goals. Others break the planning process into a series of strategic tasks with goals, timelines, and measurable results. No group is too small or too strapped financially to be media savvy.

Negative Experiences

Perhaps the only time a group's leaders have been in the spotlight has been during a problem or crisis. That kind of history can convince some leaders to avoid reporters at all costs. A bad image can be reversed with a strategic media plan, but a turnaround requires a forward-looking approach that is proactive in placing stories and that maintains a steady focus on the goal of improving the organization's image. Simply reacting and waiting for reporters to call you won't help the situation. However, with proper preparation, an organization can turn the next crisis into an opportunity. (See Chapter Eight, "Responding to a Media Crisis and Managing Backlash.")

False Assumptions

Some who are experts in their fields, heads of public agencies, scientists, scholars, researchers, and other professionals resist the notion that they have to go to the news media for attention. They assume that what they do is so important that eventually the media will come to them. Unfortunately, journalists are unlikely to seek out the silent groups when the competition for limited media space is so great.

Inexperience

There are few guides to the culture and protocols of news organizations, and people who have never dealt with reporters before may find navigating the media a frightening concept. This problem, at least, you have already begun to address with the book now in your hands.

Building a Communications Team

The first concrete step in the process of "going strategic" is to build a communications team with the best and the brightest staff, board members, and advisers you can assemble. You should not work in isolation; instead, involve organizational leaders, including top leaders and others who command respect from frontline workers as well. Look for creativity and out-of-the-box thinking among staff, volunteers, and others who can help.

Involve people who love to watch television, follow the blogging world, are regularly on the Internet, listen constantly to the radio, and read several newspapers each day. Include media-savvy people who regularly read several news Web sites, publish their own blogs, or have a presence on Web-based listservs or social networking sites. Reach out to others in the nonprofit community who might be willing to share their experiences and ideas about working with the media.

With your team assembled, you are ready to begin designing your communications strategy.

1. Spell Out Your Group's Mission

Most people working for a nonprofit have a general sense of what their group is trying to accomplish. But if you ask ten different staffers to write down a sentence explaining their group, you may get several different answers. Some organizations have conquered this first challenge of clarifying their identity by establishing a memorable tag line based on their mission.

Fundamental values can be expressed in a few words or tag line. An environmental group might stress "protecting our planet." The United Negro College Fund reminds us that "a mind is a terrible thing to waste." If your nonprofit is committed to working with others in a collaborative manner, then "partnerships for change" might describe your values. Reducing the work of talented and committed people to a bumper sticker may offend some as somehow lessening its importance. But to cut through the clutter of today's news environment, a highly distilled and memorable slogan that shapes all communications, media oriented or otherwise, will serve your organization well.

2. Choose Your Goals

Your communications goals should mirror the overall goals of your organization. These may include some or all of the following.

Goal: Enhancing Visibility and Name Recognition

Visibility and name recognition are critical to new organizations and especially important to those that have deliberately sought low profiles but now find themselves in need of public recognition. Even an established nonprofit may want to change or improve its image with a new name or logo or by highlighting redefined program areas.

The key here is to make repeated reference to your organization, whether by word of mouth, in advertising, or in news coverage. Personal interviews with community leaders, elected officials, reporters, and others can provide important perspectives of outsiders in shaping your current image, mission, and values. An Internet search of local and national news media may tell you how often your group or spokespeople are publicly mentioned.

Goal: Increasing Fundraising

Money follows programs and communications. As veteran fundraiser Roger Craver puts it, "Any group that does not have an effective communications program will raise only a fraction of the money [it] would otherwise attract."

The messages, symbols, and spokespeople that are effective in media outreach are also critical factors in successful fundraising. If your organization relies on direct mail to targeted audiences or personal letters to large donors, your appeals for donations must communicate your program goals and objectives vividly. If foundation or government grants are your main funding sources, proposals need to articulate clearly the same "who, what, when, where, why, and how" included in your press releases and information kits.

Sometimes events can do double duty. For example, celebrity AIDS walks and Race for the Cure (for breast cancer) were designed to raise money and attract media attention. Local broadcast stations and newspapers can often be persuaded to donate public service airtime and space for the recruitment of participants and to make donations through their local foundations. Major news stories can provide media and fundraising opportunities. The tragic death of Princess Diana in 1997 helped highlight groups working to ban land mines, a cause with which she was closely identified. Advocates were able to translate the massive media coverage and additional funding support into policy change at the United Nations and in dozens of countries. Natural disasters, emergency situations, and other unexpected tragedies can give your organization the opportunity to be seen in an entirely different light.

Government agencies can also benefit from media efforts, especially during appropriations and budget deliberations at the city, county, state, and federal levels. These efforts may entail rallying the support of people who benefit directly from your agency's work and working to get their stories featured in media coverage.

Goal: Reaching Influentials

Issue-oriented initiatives demand media strategies to reach "influentials," including columnists, pundits, lawmakers, and stakeholders. As a first step, decide whether you are trying to change existing public opinion or to mobilize the majority of people who already support your position. It is much harder, and more expensive, to change people's fixed attitudes than to activate supporters.

If a legislative change is your goal, you might target swing-vote elected officials, often moderates of either major party. An effort directed to editorial writers, columnists, bloggers, and news reporters, especially in the officials' home districts, can have considerable influence, possibly even making or breaking your cause.

A communications strategy for policy change allows you to frame the debate to win. Legislative efforts, by their very nature, don't require organizations to have universal support but rather to have the support of a majority. Remember, however, that media outreach activities by nonprofits that lobby are regulated under IRS rules; it is your responsibility to know which rules apply to your group.

Goal: Recruiting More Members and Volunteers

Public service efforts, paid advertising, and feature articles on your organization can motivate people to make a phone call, return a postcard, join up, renew, or volunteer. Follow-up communication, in person or in writing, is the key to keeping your core supporters active and minimizing turnover.

Whether you want to recruit foster and adoptive parents, who will have to make a major commitment of time and energy, or professionals who can give an hour a week to tutoring or participating in a local environmental cleanup, first impressions are critical. People need to feel that donating their time is as important as giving money.

Local media can be asked to become partners in your recruitment efforts, provided their participation is seen as a noncontroversial public service to the community. Many television stations, for example, run a weekly segment called Wednesday's Child as a public service to local child welfare agencies, featuring foster children who need families and are waiting to be adopted. The success of these segments, as with all recruitment efforts, depends on the agency's follow-up communications.

Goal: Reforming Public Institutions

Media organizations, especially newspapers, can be expected to take positions on issues related to education, immigration, health care, mental health, juvenile justice, or campaign finance, to name a few. From your perspective, this means that their editorial boards will be either partners in change or giant stumbling blocks.

In school districts across the country, for example, media coverage and editorial opinion have had an enormous impact on public education reform. With its crusade against large segments of a local school reform plan, a Philadelphia paper (in what many thought was an attempt to boost declining circulation) brought what one observer called "wholly unjustified charges against Philadelphia's superintendent of schools, a nationally acclaimed education reformer." The paper's attacks greatly complicated the superintendent's effort to implement his innovative, tough reform plan for the city schools. But in the Seattle area, after a northern suburban school district lost a very important bond ballot measure, a carefully devised media strategy turned the tide when the proposal was put before the voters a second time.

Goal: Improving and Increasing Service Delivery and Awareness of Public Concerns

Sometimes a communications strategy conveys a message about public behavior that explicitly tells people what to do: "Reduce, Reuse, Recycle," "Be a Designated Driver," "Tobacco-Free Kids," "Immunize Your Child," "Fight Wildfires," "Donate Blood," "Just Say No," or "Get a Mammogram." As they do with recruitment efforts, local media often will join as partners in providing important public health and service information to viewers and readers.

Goal: Turning Around Negative Media Coverage

Backlash and negative publicity demand a strategy beyond saying "No comment." Tragedies, conflicts of interest, illegal activities, and other scandals can cripple or shut down a nonprofit organization. You need to be in control of events before events control you. Communications, both internal and external, are critical and must be launched in a timely manner and to the right audiences. When dealing with the media, you must be organized, professional, and truthful. False, misleading, or ill-advised statements can do serious damage to your public image. In such times, a crisis communications plan can be your most valuable resource. (See Chapter Eight, "Responding to a Media Crisis and Managing Backlash.")

3. Commit to Being Proactive

Understand that your entire operation will need to think about the media in relation to the organization's daily work. For example, it is impossible to overstate the importance of cultivating relationships with reporters. Waiting passively for the media to call you may ensure that your group stays invisible to the outside world. Communications staff should make a regular habit of inquiring about their colleagues' work for potential story ideas.

4. Place Communications High on Your Group's Priority List

Where do good visibility and media coverage rank on your organization's list of priorities? Tensions often develop within nonprofit groups over how leaders and spokespeople spend their valuable time. How much time should managers allocate for meetings with advisers and top policy people? Administrative tasks? Consulting with board members or elected officials? Speeches to outside groups or affiliates? Fundraising? Meetings with reporters? If your group has an understanding of where media coverage fits into your overall objectives and priorities, some problems can be eased from the start.

5. Convene a Brainstorming Meeting

Whether you develop a media plan from scratch or reexamine an existing one, your top decision makers should hold an initial communications strategy session to understand just where media thinking ranks, or should rank, in the organization's workaday processes.

Have lots of poster paper handy so that ideas can be written down and hung around the room. Go around the table and ask people to outline their departments' goals. Which people do they want to reach? (In other words, who are their target audiences?) For what purposes? How important do they think communications and media relations are to achieving these goals? Ask participants to rank on a scale from 1 to 10 the value of good media coverage. If everyone gives it top priority, a 10, then ask if they will add a 0 and put 100 percent of their resources into improved communications and media relations. This usually brings a long pause.

As people rethink their commitment to communications strategies, find out what percentage of the group's overall budget now goes to media and communications. If your organization is like many nonprofits, the figure is likely to range from 10 to 20 percent. If this were a political campaign and the candidate told supporters that the media budget was that low, what do you suppose the response would be? Tell your decision makers that in most circumstances, the candidate would not be taken seriously and would have little chance of victory.

You are likely to find that the people in your group who only occasionally watch television, rarely spend time on the Internet, and only read a newspaper once in a while will give media a low priority. This reflects their limited experience with the world of media. Even people who are enthusiastic about enhanced media outreach may underestimate the resources it requires. Keep the conversation going until consensus emerges on the ranking of communications as an organizational priority. Discuss the benefits that increased visibility and media scrutiny will yield for your group, as well as the trade-offs involved. Review the overall goals of your organization, and brainstorm about the role communications might play in achieving them in such areas as fundraising, changing policy, and increasing membership.

End the session by finalizing communications goals and coming to a firm priority ranking for communications work on the 1-to-10 scale. Ask any skeptics to agree not to be roadblocks. At some point in the process, leaders will need to decide on a final communications plan, budget, and implementation process.

6. Commit the Necessary Money and Staff Time

Communications directors and press secretaries are not magicians. They need staffs, consultants, and resources for the basic activities of an effective press operation. Even if your nonprofit doesn't use paid advertising, it will need funds for enhanced Web sites, audio press conferences, and express mail. It will also need funds to produce graphics, develop and maintain press lists, cultivate relationships with reporters, develop and manage Web site content, and produce printed materials and news feeds.

Moreover, responsibility for developing the communications plan and for cultivating regular press coverage should not rest exclusively with a communications staff or volunteer committee. Your lead spokesperson, usually the executive director, president, or agency director, must be involved in the planning.

Your media effort may be as simple and inexpensive as regular conversations or meetings with journalists. As Marcy Whitebook, director of the Center for the Study of Child Care Employment in Berkeley, California, describes her work with reporters, "I make a point of being a reliable source, and we always return phone calls promptly. After beating the bushes for coverage, reporters now regularly call us, in large part because we are always accessible." She also understands that not all media contacts turn into immediate stories. It takes time to develop good working relationships. And "personal relationships are a must," Whitebook points out. After years of regular media cultivation, she now has a computer database full of the names of editors and reporters whom she knows personally and who regularly file stories about her center's work. She also has a stack of good media clips and clippings to show for it.

The more money and resources your organization can devote to media relations, the more coverage you will receive. If your leaders decide that media coverage is a high priority, then they must be prepared to allocate not only financial resources but also their personal energies and time. They need to help plan and implement media strategies, make public appearances, do interviews, and participate in sessions that analyze coverage.

If media coverage is agreed to be relatively important but is seen on a par with other internal concerns of your organization, the communications and media relations staff must be included in overall organizational planning. A creative, energetic communications staff with the ability and commitment to promote the organization can mean the difference between the success and failure of your mission and goals.

Chapter 2

Elements of a Strategic Communications Plan

- Build on a foundation of goals, vision, and values.
- Target audiences, conduct research, marshal resources, and create a work plan.
- Implement day-to-day activities.

THE ELEMENTS OF a communications plan are basically the same whether you are a small advocacy group, a large not-for-profit hospital, a museum, a university, a service provider, or a foundation. This chapter briefly introduces those elements (discussed in detail in later chapters) and includes a case study of their successful use in the recent Fairness Initiative on Low-Wage Work. But before we move into the elements of a strategic communications plan, it helps to understand how issues move from obscurity to prominence.

How Issues Move Up the Media Food Chain

To the extent that any nonprofit group or government agency exists to further the public good, it is concerned with some kind of issue, even if it does not grab daily headlines or generate controversy. Important high-profile issues generally start as smaller ones, grow larger in predictable and sometimes manageable stages, and affect public opinion in observable ways.

This was the case with the Fairness Initiative on Low-Wage Work, which had its origin in city and state efforts to increase minimum wages, arcing from a local business story to the state politics page and then to national coverage.

FIGURE 2.1

Issues Media Curve: How Issues Move Through the Media

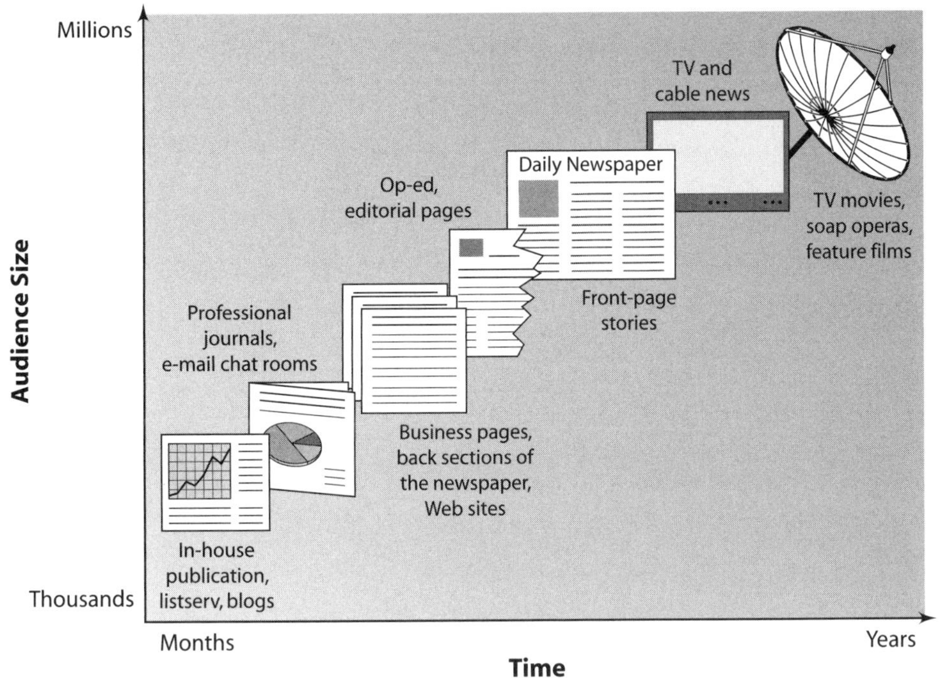

When such stories leapfrog their way to prominence, it is usually because of their impact on people and families. There has also been a huge increase in television news coverage of research published in professional journals. And the advent of the Internet makes it possible for stories posted on the Web site of a previously obscure organization to get worldwide circulation in minutes. Despite those developments, in most cases, the issues media curve we first identified in the 1980s (Figure 2.1) continues to be a useful model of the development of public awareness and opinion. Stories start small and get larger in a fairly consistent manner:

1. New ideas and policies usually first appear on the pages of in-house publications (such as corporate or organizational e-newsletters), in speeches and papers presented at professional or academic gatherings, in the policy-oriented forums of universities or think tanks, in the e-mail notices sent to subscribers of small Internet listservs, or in personal blogs. At this stage, the audience for the issue may number a few dozen to a few hundred specialists.

2. Nationally circulated professional journals, specialty or trade books, commercial newsletters, Internet chat rooms, super and mainstream bloggers, and scientific magazines can also launch, or build support for, new developments or ideas. Perhaps ten thousand people may be aware of a story at this point.

3. Beat reporters (assigned by mainstream news organizations to cover specific topics) monitor journals, blogs, and events for news of wider interest. Health and human services reporters may read social service professionals' publications to spot emerging trends; legal reporters read law journals for story ideas; and auto industry reporters read specialty newsletters to stay informed. Specialized Web sites may also be a source. Press coverage of the trend or issue often appears in the metro news or business sections of the daily newspaper.

4. Over time, reported developments attract the attention of editorial writers, who shape a newspaper's official position on the issue. This position might come in the form of an endorsement of a candidate, support for passage of legislation, or simply a comment on local events. Relevant viewpoints and commentary start to appear, written by regular columnists or by outside contributors. These articles and editorials are opinion pieces, but they often set the stage for direct action.

5. It usually takes breaking news or a major event, such as a Supreme Court ruling, an election, a natural disaster, or a major state government action, to catapult an issue to the front or home page or to the lead story on national news. More and more, newspapers are softening their Page One approach to include features that in the past would have been found only in one of the back sections.

6. Network television newscasts often take their cue from the front and home pages of national dailies, updating stories that appeared in the morning papers with their own coverage of the day's events. In the absence of a breaking story—such as a trial verdict or a natural disaster—those updates may form a substantial part of the nightly news. At this point, the story has reached millions of Americans.

7. After the concept or issue has been thoroughly aired in increasingly influential media, it may enter pop culture in the form of made-for-television movies, special television events, reality shows, and feature films.

• • •

A communications strategy must also consider the interplay between coverage and public opinion. For example, during the early stages of an issue's coverage, the public may harbor conflicting opinions or, more likely, no opinions at all. Depending on the amount of press coverage of a group or an issue, your organization may find that the undecided people are more important targets than the opinion elite, who read key sections of the newspaper, including editorials and columnists' pieces. Knowing how to target the undecided middle is largely a product of understanding how people, information, and events shape public opinion.

Against this background, it should be clear that news or entertainment coverage of issues and organizations rarely just happens. It is a function of the conscientious efforts of interested parties to cultivate reporters and educate target audiences, the public, and the policymakers.

Key Principles

A communications plan affirms and is driven by (1) your organization's goals and outcomes; (2) its vision, as expressed in a mission statement; and (3) its values and beliefs.

If your nonprofit or public agency is planning to launch a communications plan, you need to start by addressing some fundamental questions:

- Does the public already support the goals of your organization? If so, then the challenge is to marshal the resources needed to mobilize people.
- Is there so much opposition that an effort must first be mounted to form or change public opinion? Is there a general lack of awareness of the group and its goals and issues?
- What is the appropriate communications strategy, given the level of public understanding?

In addition to establishing goals based on your mission and values, there are six critical elements to building a communications strategy:

1. An understanding of your target audience and how to reach it
2. Research into past media coverage and public opinion about your issues
3. Messages to be delivered
4. Materials to be produced
5. Resources from which staff and equipment will be drawn
6. A written work plan, which incorporates ongoing activities for achieving or maintaining communications goals

The importance of identifying these elements and putting them in place before implementing day-to-day activities cannot be overstated. Outcomes will be determined by your success at pulling these six elements together.

FIGURE 2.2

Strategic Communications Planning Guide

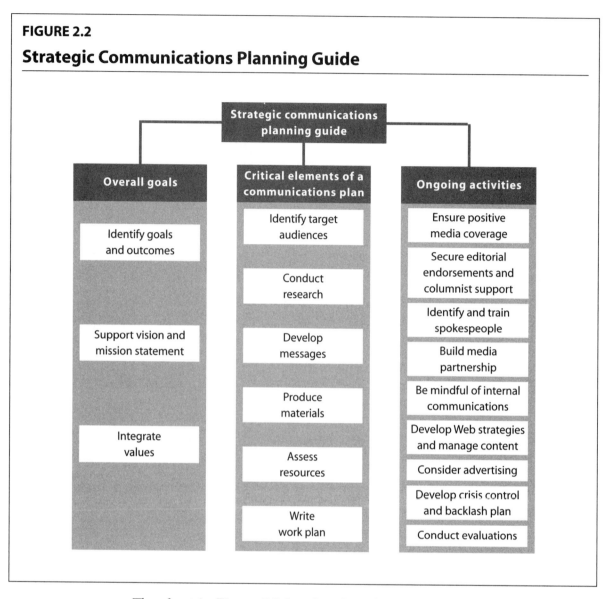

The chart in Figure 2.2 is a handy reference tool and should serve as a guide to your strategic communications planning. We review the overall goals and the six elements one by one in the next sections to give you a sense of how a targeted communications strategy works, and later chapters discuss them in much greater detail.

Set Overall Communications Goals

Goals are good, but they must also be measurable so that you can gauge progress along the way and know when you have achieved them. If, for example, your goal is to recruit more members, state how many you intend to attract. If you want to raise awareness about an issue, decide how you will measure success. Will it be by responses to a Web site? Through an increase in the number of services provided? Media contacts?

If your organization has only been reactive in its dealings with reporters, it may be time for a proactive effort that includes a minimum number of press events, meetings with reporters, or briefings that support your organization's overall communications goals.

Create a Vision and Mission Statement

Your organizational mission statement will be the cornerstone of your communications plan, driving the overall direction of your media activities. Include this mission statement at the very beginning of your communications plan to remind staff, board members, and other internal decision makers that media-related activities flow from the core mission and vision of the organization, not just from its communications department. Do not let media outreach cause you to lose sight of the bigger picture. Make sure that "what you stand for" is reflected in all your media activities.

Integrate Organizational Values and Beliefs

Every organization, foundation, public agency, and institution has at its heart a system of values and beliefs. Unlike opinions, which can shift in a short period, values are long lasting. They emerge in the context of conflicts over government versus individual rights, individual freedoms versus group responsibility, and diversity versus tradition.

Everything stems from those core values; they are the organization's reason for being and should be reflected in any new plans and goals the organization creates, including communications goals. For example, the Annie E. Casey Foundation of Baltimore firmly believes that "children do best in families"; its grantmaking and communications plans support this. The Sierra Club's slogan "Explore, enjoy and protect our planet" clearly states its values and aligns the organization unequivocally with the primary environmental connections of most Americans.

Identify Your Target Audiences

One of the first steps in devising a communications plan is to determine who your target audiences are and how to reach them. List categories of people who are important to the success of your communications effort. Identify the media they consume and whose word they will respect. What kinds of stories are those particular people likely to read in the newspaper, watch on television and cable, view on the Internet, or listen to on the radio?

A Word About Branding

In recent years, many foundations and nonprofit organizations have focused on branding as part of their overall communications plans. As an advertising device, branding has a long history. For example, the Advertising Council and the U.S. Forest Service began using the slogan "Only you can prevent forest fires" in the 1940s. It has been updated to "Only you can prevent wildfires." Through successful branding efforts, the National Association for Stock Car Auto Racing (NASCAR) has made itself synonymous with auto racing, IBM with business solutions, and Apple with innovation. Even company names have come to have their own lexicon—for example, Google as a synonym for Web search.

Branding is an attempt to define a single organization or its activities as a unique brand. Commonly used to individualize commercial products ranging from soap to automobiles, it can also be used by non-profits. Organizations may adopt a slogan to distinguish themselves from others, or try to make the point more powerfully with paid advertising. The key here is the availability of resources to provide the drumbeat for a repetitive and, to the extent possible, universal paid advertising campaign. It is much more difficult for an earned media plan to succeed in branding an organization or advocacy effort. There is another challenge to branding (apart from the high cost). The most successful advocacy efforts in the nonprofit world tend to involve the collaboration of many different groups working toward the same objective. The use of branding to uniquely characterize a particular organization within the coalition may foster competition or promote the hoarding of proprietary information, defeating the purpose of the joint effort, in which the groups downplay their individual identities.

In summary, branding is generally not effective in collaborative situations and usually requires a sizable budget for paid advertising.

Keep in mind that with so many segmented and specialized media now in operation, the concept of a "general public" hardly exists anymore, and may include current donors, prospective members or recruits, elected officials, church groups, judges and the legal community, health care providers, journalists, business leaders, communities of color, trade associations, women's leaders, teens, senior citizens, and the cross-cutting category of "influentials."

The key to understanding how to target your audiences is that you almost never have to communicate to the entire public all at once; rather, you need to focus on carefully chosen segments or, in the case of policymakers and other influential people, a very narrow slice of the population.

With this in mind, it helps to have as much information as possible about existing media audiences. Fortunately, media outlets can often supply data on the size and demographics of their readership or viewing audiences, typically packaged as marketing information for advertisers, at no cost. This can be especially helpful as you begin media placement efforts with reporters and editors.

Do not forget your internal audiences: make sure your staff, board members, volunteers, and other key supporters within and outside your organization are clear about your communications goals and who will deliver the messages.

Conduct Research into Media Coverage, Public Opinion, and Supporting Facts

How are your organization and issues perceived by those you seek to influence? Through Internet searches and with the help of Web-based resources, you can develop an instructive profile of how your issues are covered in the media, how often your organization is quoted, how others describe it, and what public opinion polls have been conducted on relevant topics. A straightforward, multiyear analysis of your organization's media coverage will suggest the amount of resources needed to achieve your communications goals.

Part of your communications plan should be to collect data on your issues in formats that reporters and editors can easily use to answer the "who, what, when, where, why, and how" in every story. A side benefit to that approach is that it transforms the data you need to help shape communications into a virtual gold mine in your outreach to reporters. Begin by categorizing all available internal data according to their usefulness to journalists, and when the time comes to answer their questions, you will be well prepared.

Develop Messages

If you had to write just a few words to describe your recent work, what would it say? One way to start developing messages is to imagine you are looking at tomorrow's edition of your daily newspaper. What headline about your organization would you want to see—"Paid Family Leave Becoming a Reality in California," "Health Care for All Approved," or "Study Shows Clearer Air and Cleaner Water"?

Work back from this headline to fill in the missing elements: Who made this happen? What obstacles did they encounter? Why is this important to others in the community and throughout the country? What role did your organization play? These are the things you would want to tell the reporter who was writing this article. And think visually. What possible photographs or creative video can be supplied with the story?

Another important activity that should come early in the process of developing messages is to establish how to state your group's goals succinctly and to say in a few words how the group wants to be described. It is a question that often arises at the end of interviews, and if you fail to offer a brief and ready response, journalists will come up with their own, potentially inaccurate, tag line for your organization.

Once you have settled on core messages and supporting points, a useful exercise for staying on message is to develop a "message box" with "talking points" for your spokespeople to use whenever they talk to reporters. The box contains your key or central point, and around it are supporting facts, a call to action, and other secondary messages. (Chapter Four discusses the message box in greater detail.) Thinking in terms of a box, rather than a list, can help you remember to jump back to the central argument throughout the interview.

With the message box in mind, take time to answer the following question in-house before every media event or interview: What do you want the ensuing headline and pictures to look like? Imagine the best, and start each interview with the premise that it can be achieved.

Also do this exercise in reverse. Ask yourself what the worst possible headline or visual could be. If your bill were defeated or if angry group members were to denounce your organization publicly, what could you say to the media to put that in perspective? And no matter what questions you are asked, use every opportunity to deliver your key points.

Limit your messages to three or four key points that you want to communicate in each interview. Remember, if your talking points are complicated and hard to understand, then it's unlikely that your spokespeople will ever be able to explain your messages in clear, concise language.

Produce High-Quality Public Relations Materials

Your public relations materials are important tools for reaching reporters, donors, policymakers, influentials, and others in your target group. Your toolbox should include the following:

- A good logo and stationery design that will last awhile; the logo should be easy to read in an electronic format
- An easy-to-understand, one-page fact sheet about your organization
- At least one press kit on the issues and activities you want to highlight to the media, with a one-page fact sheet on each
- Brochures that can be printed on paper and adapted for a Web site
- Photos, videos, slides, overheads, and computer presentations that tell your story
- Reports and studies for public release as news items
- Short bios of your leaders and spokespeople
- Your current newsletter, if there is one
- Copies of published articles or Web features about your group

All of these should be produced in formats that can be posted to your Web site. Design your Web site to include a separate and clearly marked media or "press room" button on your home page; also include "press" hyperlinks on all pages.

Keep your audience in mind when designing Web sites or print publications. You do not want your press kit to suggest that you have enormous resources to splurge on expensive paper stock or embossing, separate color photos, and die cuts if you are working to reduce poverty. Likewise, a clearly organized Web site that is searchable and user-friendly is more important than one with high production values. The right place on the design continuum is somewhere between slick and tacky.

Assess Resources

Spell out how you will allocate staff time, budgets, computers, databases, in-house and contract services, and volunteer or intern help. A communications, public affairs, or media director is a must for midsize to large organizations. In agencies with fewer than ten employees or volunteers, everyone from the executive director to the person who answers the phone should be a part of the communications team. A resource review should do the following:

- Assess staff time, in-house services, and existing media technologies.

- Recommend and arrange for training and technology upgrades as needed.

- Designate or hire someone to be responsible for communications.

- Develop a budget that includes provisions for such outside services as freelance writing, video production, database management, graphic design, and Web site management.

- Build or expand access to executive loan programs, internships, pro bono media support, donations, and grants. (See Chapter Six, "Making the Most of Your Resources.")

Write a Work Plan for Ongoing Outreach and Related Activities

Specific strategies for winning positive media coverage, editorial endorsements, or media partnerships are as varied as the media landscape and the communities you serve, but the elements of a basic media plan are fairly constant. What follows are nine fairly typical communications goals and functions, along with suggested ongoing activities for achieving or maintaining them. Use this list as a menu from which to adopt or modify activities for your specific situation. (You will find an in-depth discussion of tips and tactics in Chapter Seven, "Earning Good Media Coverage.")

1. Ensure Positive Media Coverage

Positive stories in the media are earned through an investment of funds and resources over time. The term *earned media* is now widely used to describe what used to be called public relations or "free media" (as opposed to paid media or advertising). If your organization or agency is already newsworthy or can make news, develop a strategy for regular positive news coverage. Here's how:

- Cultivate personal relationships with reporters, editors, and media gatekeepers.
- Develop a calendar of events around key issues or activities, such as the release of a report.
- Plan and initiate additional news events to expand media coverage opportunities.
- Coordinate written materials for print media, develop visuals for photographers and broadcasters, and make tapes for audio news feeds.
- Schedule press conferences sparingly and media briefings when warranted.
- Distribute press releases on significant developments by fax, mail, e-mail, or hand delivery.
- Update your Web site with new information and materials on a regular basis.

Feature stories or "softer" news items about people, places, and issues attract diverse audiences and tend to be "evergreen"; in other words, they do not have the urgency or timeliness of "hard" breaking news. To pitch a feature piece to a reporter, outline your desired approach to the story before you call. Don't get discouraged. It may take several tries and different story ideas before a reporter responds positively. Also, the increasing use of voice mail means that you may have to try several times to reach reporters with your pitch.

Writing articles for publication and scheduling broadcast or cable appearances on public affairs programming featuring your spokespeople are good ways to get your messages across in their purest form, without a reporter's interpretation. Try the following:

- Write and place bylined opinion articles or op-eds in newspapers.
- Coordinate timely, sharp, and relevant letters to the editor.

- Join Internet media Web sites for chats and instant responses.
- Schedule regular appearances on talk radio and television public affairs shows.
- Offer comments on news developments to producers of news and newsmagazine shows. They may be interested in having your spokesperson discuss them on the air.

2. Secure Editorial Endorsements and Columnist Support

Newspapers and many local news programs take positions on issues and endorse or participate in nonprofit activities such as walkathons. The *New York Times,* for example, runs a yearly winter holiday series called the Neediest Cases, with specific examples chosen by the seven agencies supporting a *Times*-administered fund by the same name.

To attain editorial support for your group or issue,

- Set up face-to-face editorial board meetings at daily, weekly, or neighborhood papers. Be prepared to *ask* the editorial board to take a position on the editorial page; that is their job, and the arguments and data you provide can help them decide.
- Generate mailings, e-mails, and faxes with clips and fact sheets about your issue or activity, along with requests for support.
- Send columnists your story ideas and opinions about issues that they may want to address.

3. Identify Spokespeople and Train Them in Media Skills

Being interviewed successfully, especially in front of a camera, is a learned skill. No one, repeat no one, should just wing it with on-air reporters. Practicing before a home video camera can be an effective way of making sure your messages get across; that your posture, gestures, and clothing are not distracting; and that your overall manner is persuasive and articulate.

At a minimum, make sure that spokespeople for your organization and any others likely to be talking to reporters receive some professional training. (See Chapter Nine, "Selecting and Training Spokespeople," for tips on media training.)

4. Build Media Partnerships

Always remember that the news media are businesses first. They are major corporations with stockholders' interests firmly in mind, and they want to build audiences and sell advertising. Your organization may be in a position to help them do both.

The less controversial your organization is, the more willing a media outlet will be to forge a partnership with you. Across the country, media have provided institutional support for worthy causes, with events ranging from lengthy broadcast telethons to fifteen-second public service announcements. Some mount impressive multipart or episodic campaigns that give viewers and readers information about major current issues, such as health care or child welfare. Others promote community activities or other free services on their news programs or pages. Media personalities volunteer time and money.

The *Washington Post,* for example, joined efforts to help reform District of Columbia schools by offering summer training programs for teachers. The *Post*'s local foundation also makes grants to community groups and organizations in the arts and to organizations that help minorities advance in the fields of journalism and communications.

In another partnership, the repercussions of which are still being felt many years later, the Charles H. Revson Foundation sponsored and extended the audience of a 1996 television series aimed at changing the religious dialogue in America. *Genesis: A Living Conversation* was hosted by Bill Moyers, who used the Bible to promote tolerance of religious differences, saying that the conversation had for too long been dominated by the "religious right." To stimulate interfaith Bible study in hundreds of communities across the country, the foundation distributed one hundred thousand copies of *Talking About Genesis,* a teaching guide for groups and families, which was also available in bookstores and through WNET's Web site. Earned media coverage included a *Time* cover story, dozens of national radio and television appearances by Moyers, and headlines in most of the country's leading newspapers.

Public service advertising can also be an important way to reach your target audiences. You can use the local calendar of events sections in newspapers and on radio and television to provide information to audiences about your events and to enhance your organization's name recognition.

Media partnerships might include

- Public service announcements (PSAs) that advertise events, recruit members, explain service delivery, and build the organization's image
- National and local documentaries or feature films
- Billboard and transit campaigns on buses and subways
- Agreements by advertisers to "barter" space in the media in order to help your cause

5. Be Mindful of Internal Communications

Staff members, boards of directors, and volunteers can be your best assets. But they need regularly updated information about what your organization is doing. Otherwise, they cannot accurately represent your cause to friends, family, neighbors, and others in their circles of influence. When it comes to working with the media, your team also needs to be trained and ready to deal with press calls and inquiries. This applies as much to the receptionist who answers the phone as to your top spokespeople.

6. Develop Web Strategies and Manage Content

An organization's Web site often must serve several audiences, including people who are learning about the group for the first time, researchers and others looking for expertise and commentary, and those who want to stay up-to-date on the group's activities and accomplishments. Great care should go into strategic decisions about what the Web site is intended to do. For example, a site might serve as an archive of research products, compile and digest media reports on a key topic, provide individual commentary by bloggers, or offer some combination of these.

In any case, content on the site should be managed in a way that keeps the site fresh for its intended audience. This may require daily revisions to the home page for an advocacy group involved in developing issues, or less frequent changes for a charity that reports mainly on internal developments. Part of the overall strategy for the site should include constant testing of its features and the audience's response to them, often measured as "click-throughs" (in this case, the number of times readers click to a new page to learn more or take action).

7. Consider Paid Advertising

Buying media time or space guarantees that your messages will be delivered in the exact words you choose and to your target audiences. In 2006, U.S. businesses invested $340 billion in paid advertising. Politicians running for office typically spend 50 to 75 percent of their campaign funds on advertising.

Investing in advertising is an art, not necessarily a science. Most nonprofits and government agencies simply do not have the resources to spend on paid media. If you do, you might also want to invest in an agency that knows how to make your ads vibrant. Use this book to keep tabs on that advertising agency and to make sure you are getting the skilled work you have paid for. See Chapter Eleven, "Chapters Online," for an introduction to the online chapter dedicated to paid advertising and PSAs.

8. Develop a Crisis Control and Backlash Plan

Regardless of how noncontroversial you think your organization, agency, or issues may be, prepare for a crisis or backlash in the media. Don't get caught by surprise. Plan for the worst possible headlines or story, and agree beforehand how your group will control events, in a worst-case scenario, before the situation becomes a media stampede.

Think of your crisis control plan as a fire drill. It is preparation for an emergency that can erupt at any time but that also may never happen at all. Here are three critical pieces (also see Chapter Eight, "Responding to a Media Crisis and Managing Backlash"):

- Identify a crisis coordination team.
- Develop a special communications plan to ensure timely and appropriate responses.
- Conduct internal briefings about implementing damage control procedures.

9. Conduct Evaluation and Establish Accountability

Every strategic plan should have an integral evaluation component to establish accountability and make improvements over time. Major activities might include analyzing media content and monitoring certain developments, such as shifts in public opinion, policy changes, increased memberships and organizational participation, and improved institutional capacity. Chapter Eleven, "Chapters Online," introduces further discussion of this topic and an online chapter covering evaluation; and CCMC's Web site dedicated to evaluation, www.mediaevaluationproject.org, goes into extensive detail with respect to media evaluation.

Case Study: The Fairness Initiative on Low-Wage Work

Each year in the late summer, the Census Bureau releases a report on poverty in the United States. And each year, the report gets front-page headlines for a day or two in newspapers across the country, along with mentions of modest length on the nightly news. The coverage is always focused on the numbers: whether the proportion of people living in poverty has risen or fallen over the preceding year. Except for a few newspaper editorials, there is scant coverage of deeper issues, such as the causes of poverty, or of the policy debate on how to solve them.

In 2005, the aftermath of Hurricane Katrina brought new urgency to public concerns about poverty. Saturation coverage of the post-Katrina tragedy allowed millions of Americans to see that hundreds of thousands of people live close to the edge, in extreme poverty. The breech of the New Orleans levees and ensuing flood uncovered a larger challenge to society along the Gulf Coast.

But within weeks of the storm's passage, the urgency brought about by Katrina started to fade, and with it the focus on remedies for poverty. A catastrophic tsunami in Asia turned the world's focus away from New Orleans. For a time, it seemed that a historic "teachable moment" in American society might pass with little impact, becoming just another piece of old news.

That was the concern of a collaborative coalition that had been working since 2001 to conduct media outreach and public education on the systemic problems Katrina later exposed. The case of the Fairness Initiative on Low-Wage Work is worth examining, as it employed the key elements of a successful strategic communications plan: research on the best ways to frame the debate, coordinated outreach based on consistent themes, and targeted state and regional efforts in which members of the twenty-group collaborative joined forces to have significant national impact. And it had the desired impact: the Initiative laid the foundation for the passage in 2007 of an increase in the federal minimum wage, the first in a decade.

The collaboration involved activist groups, such as ACORN, the Center for Community Change, the Center for Law and Social Policy, and the National Partnership for Women & Families; research organizations, such as the Economic Policy Institute, the Institute for Women's Policy Research, and the National Center for Children in Poverty; and other groups, including the AFL-CIO, the Workforce Alliance, and Wider Opportunities for Women. With support from the Ford, Russell Sage, Nathan Cummings, and Annie E. Casey Foundations and the Rockefeller Family Fund, the Initiative eventually addressed a spectrum of related issues—among them, the minimum wage, health care reform, paid sick days, paid family leave, and enhanced adult job training.

Among its early steps in 2001 was an extensive program of research on perceptions about the working poor, those American families with one or more employed adult living below the poverty line. An initial analysis of themes in media coverage found a "fix the person" model to be prevalent. That is, the root of poverty was perceived to be the failure of individuals to better their own lives.

The research found that the strongest alternative argument, what strategists call the "frame," recast poverty as a failure of society at large to create an economy that supports families and strengthens communities. Such a frame shifted the focus away from the failures of "working poor" individuals to the need for "an economy that works for all." A key concept behind this line of reasoning was that the economy is not a force of nature, beyond human control, but the product of past decisions and policies.

In its first year, the Fairness Initiative established a system of regular communications among its collaborators, which built the working relationships needed to begin a national media strategy. The group and its outside experts developed background materials on low-wage work and its remedies, and media outreach began.

A Collaborative Approach

The Initiative established a structure that ensured maximum participation by all its members, from the earliest stages of research and strategy design through the final elements of its implementation. Involving all twenty groups in the research resulted in early agreement about target audiences and opinion leaders. Simple messages and theme lines were tested and refined. Every group was involved in every step, so all were invested in the messages to be employed. The groups met regularly to develop communications plans and to train members to speak with a consistent voice.

Emotionally Appealing and Positive Messages

Douglas Gould and Company (DG&C) and Meg Bostrom of Public Knowledge were engaged to conduct extensive opinion research on how to best frame the issues. DG&C brought together a diverse advisory group of academics, activists, and grantees, who developed a list of possible public policies to help "working poor" families.

Their analysis began with a review of media coverage for the six-month period between February 1, 2001, and July 31, 2001. Articles and editorials were examined to determine attitudes toward low-wage work and people employed in low-wage work and living in poverty. In its report, DG&C found that radio and television coverage simply tuned out the situation of people in low-wage jobs: they were largely invisible. When newspapers did write about them, it was normally in the metro section, not in the main news section, and it cast those in low-wage work as sympathetic individuals stuck in a bad situation, falling behind and unable to climb the economic ladder. Media specialists speculated that the short-sightedness of this coverage stemmed not from any hostility on the editors' part to the plight of the working poor, but from their judgment that these issues were of little concern to their readers.

With this analysis in hand, DG&C and Bostrom looked at public opinion data on issues related to poverty and upward mobility, including perceptions of the poor. Their 2001 meta-analysis (a study of previously conducted opinion research) suggested that past efforts to address poverty had been hampered by insufficient attention to the following core American beliefs:

- Each individual is responsible for his or her own success or failure.

- With hard work comes reward.

- The goal is equal opportunity, not equal outcome.

- Anyone can achieve the American Dream.

A further study found it more effective to place root solutions to poverty in the context of the overall economy, the nature of capitalism, and the potential for prosperity, rather than in a separate world occupied only by the poor. Most Americans' top-of-the-mind model of the economy is that of a "free market" that should be unconstrained and free of government intervention. If that opinion is allowed to take hold, policies to assist people in low-wage work can be attacked as inappropriate government intervention. But if an alternative model of the economy is put forward, those attacks lose force.

This alternative framing led to messages about poverty as an economic issue linked to the broad values of shared responsibility and the social importance of planning for the future. A 2002 report authored by DG&C and Bostrom, based on a national survey of registered voters, found that this framing could lead to a highly effective message about the need for planning responsibly and making investments in society today in order to produce an economy that works for all. This study also found that the best frame was one that shifted the focus away from low-wage workers to low-wage work itself. By putting the spotlight on the work itself, rather than the workers, the frame gets around the tendency to blame the victims. At the same time, many American families had friends or family members with college degrees who were working in low-wage jobs with no health care or retirement packages. Thus the new messages supported the actual life experiences of many target audiences.

In sum, the DG&C and Bostrom analysis found that the Fairness Initiative should

- Start the discussion with a focus on values, not specific policies

- Focus on work, not on individual workers or on "sympathy for the poor" stories

- Stress that the economy is not a force of nature but the product of previous decisions, and that policymakers regularly make adjustments in our economy to benefit one group over another
- Speak in terms of ways to plan our economy so that it works for all Americans
- Focus on compelling stories that illuminate systemic problems and solutions
- Include grantees and activist organizations in the development of overall frames and key message points

Training Spokespeople

Successful strategies require articulate, respected messengers for public presentations and interviews with print and electronic journalists, so the initiative coordinated more than fifty workshops with potential spokespeople across the country drawn from the ranks of advocates, academia, and people in low-wage work themselves. Spokespeople were coached in half-day and one-day sessions that incorporated the most important and effective communications techniques, from on-camera training to highlighting the common messages of the communications strategy.

A Rapid Response System

As new research findings and reports about low-wage work appeared in the media, the Fairness Initiative provided all its collaborating organizations with twice-weekly electronic news clips of top stories and articles about these issues. This allowed quick responses to events. For example, immediately after receiving reports that several business organizations in Arizona had released a report decrying the passage of a state-based minimum wage, advocates released data from the Economic Policy Institute in rebuttal.

Participants also received occasional one- or two-page memos containing media talking points on important new reports, which equipped them to respond to the media in a coordinated way and often served as templates for op-ed pieces and speeches.

Cultivating the Media

Recognizing the importance of media outreach in any communications strategy, the Fairness Initiative began regular efforts to pitch stories to reporters and producers, with an emphasis on national and regional publications.

Initiative members also were coached on how to draft op-ed articles for local and national newspapers. In all their outreach, these messengers stuck close to the key message points that were developed for the strategy to call attention to their organizations' major events. The Initiative regularly evaluated press coverage of low-wage work issues and built a master media database with state-by-state break-outs of about fifteen hundred reporters, editors, and publishers nationwide, which was made available to all Initiative participants.

Developing Materials

All collaborating organizations worked together to develop and disseminate a comprehensive media and information kit for reporters and policymakers, which was sent to hundreds of reporters and local affiliates of member organizations.

Providing Technical Assistance

Ongoing help in summarizing research, crafting specific talking points for local developments, and so on proved paramount to sustaining the organizations and the communications strategy itself.

Developing a Web Site

The Fairness Initiative Web site, http://lowwagework.org, had multiple purposes: to inform the media about low-wage work issues in much the same way as the information kit, and to provide groups working on low-wage work issues across the country with up-to-date information about the Initiative and its issues.

The Web site's first page told "the story" of low-wage work, with emphasis on the enormity of the challenge and a few generic solutions. Other sections of the Web site included

- Scores of recent reports on low-wage work, indexed by more than a dozen subject areas
- Contact information for more than three dozen low-wage work experts, listed by subject area
- The top five newspaper stories on low-wage work issues appearing across the country, updated on a weekly basis
- A series of podcasts on low-wage work issues by experts in the field
- Important press releases on low-wage work issues from collaborating organizations

Moving Up the Media Food Chain:
The *Oprah Winfrey* Show

In spring 2006, Oprah Winfrey highlighted the plight of people in low-wage work and their families in a special sixty-minute program that reached millions of people. The show featured a documentary on people struggling to get by on the minimum wage and an interview with low-wage work expert Beth Shulman from the Fairness Initiative.

Shulman presented the case for an increase in the minimum wage in a values-oriented way that stressed fairness, the need to provide for self-reliance in the economy, and strengthening the family.

Sustainability

One of the main objectives of the Initiative was sustainability. Large organizations in the collaborative, such as the AFL-CIO and the Economic Policy Institute, have capable communications staff to carry out their own media plans. But smaller member groups and grassroots organizations, such as ACORN, the Institute for Women's Policy Research, and the Workforce Alliance, have few full-time or even part-time communications specialists. It was therefore important to help train key personnel to implement strategies on their own. This was accomplished by "lessons learned" sessions at quarterly meetings of the collaborative and through coaching with individual groups preparing to release their own low-wage work reports.

Larger groups in the collaborative also helped the smaller groups with their communications needs.

Evaluation

After the first two years of media outreach by the Fairness Initiative, DG&C performed a second comprehensive review of media coverage to evaluate progress on how often low-wage work issues were covered and how they were portrayed. The study found that the term "low-wage work" was being used much more frequently than disempowering terms like "low-income worker"; it attributed the increase in positive news coverage to the Fairness Initiative and found that overall coverage of those issues had also increased substantially.

On the policy side, the federal minimum wage has been increased for the first time in ten years, and new legislation has been introduced to provide paid sick days as a minimum standard for many workers.

Chapter 3
Conducting Research and Targeting Audiences

- Know whom to inform, persuade, or mobilize.
- Monitor public opinion.
- Find out what the target audience knows and who effective messengers are.

AS THE FAIRNESS Initiative case study illustrated in Chapter Two, once the values and goals of a strategic communications plan are established, you need to ask several key questions. First, who are the target audiences you are trying to reach? Next, is the purpose of the communications plan to inform key audiences about your issue or organization and raise awareness? Or is it to enhance the importance of an issue or group? Are you asking people to take some kind of action? Finally, who are the most effective messengers, and what are the messages that will resonate the most with your target audiences?

Defining Target Audiences

Whom do you want to reach? If, for example, the main objective is to use the media to support your fundraising efforts, then your target audience might include large donors, appropriations committees of state legislatures, budget committees of a city council, foundation leaders, or select residents of a specific neighborhood or town. To reach potential large donors, you are likely to target adults with higher incomes and a history of making contributions. Articles in an Ivy League college alumni magazine or the *Wall Street Journal* could fit the bill. If, by contrast, you are building a program for teens, consider posting messages on the Web sites of teen magazines or on social networking sites such as MySpace or Facebook in order to reach them.

An Audience of One

On occasion, the target of a specific communications strategy can be a single individual. In one large mid-western state, the head of a key legislative committee was known to drive himself on a weekly schedule from his rural district to the state capital—a five-hour trip. Strategists made saturation buys of radio ads on stations along this legislator's commuting route. Although the costs for purchasing rural radio were low, the heavy buy of small-town stations gave the impression of a massive strategy reaching from one end of the state to the other.

Your media planning should include at least one brainstorming session on target audiences, with breakdowns for age, race, ethnicity, political party affiliation, marital status, and so on. If the list grows unwieldy, try grouping categories into clusters, or develop primary and secondary lists of targets.

Segments or clusters might include the following:

- Women who are employed part-time with small children (categorized by sex, occupation, marital status, and income). This cluster may be highly motivated to take action on issues related to children, early care and education, health and safety.

- Ninth-grade science teachers (categorized by education, geography, and age). This cluster may have an interest in environmental issues or school reform.

- Program officers at midsize foundations in your city (categorized by geography, education, and income). This cluster of potential donors is likely to read a local daily newspaper, the *New York Times,* and the *Chronicle of Philanthropy* and to listen to NPR.

If you are using the media to recruit members or activists, consider conducting focus group discussions or surveying your existing members to determine their interests and group them into a manageable number of different clusters. You can perform your own market research with a small investment of time. For example, if you represent a children's agency that is looking for adoptive or foster parents, ask the existing pool of foster parents about their media habits and how they were recruited.

Understanding Cluster Analysis

A cluster analysis can be understood as a computer-aided application of the old adage, "Birds of a feather flock together." This kind of analysis is based on data from surveys with many variables, including demographic (sex, age, income, education) and lifestyle characteristics (hobbies, level of social engagement, consumer behavior). It has been applied to commercial market research for at least three decades, and has had adherents in the social marketing field for nearly as long.

To get a quick sense of how cluster analysis works, visit the Web site of the market research firm Claritas (http://claritas.com/claritas/segmentation.jsp). There you can plug in any ZIP code to generate that area's top market segments. Claritas has distinctive and proprietary labels for over a hundred different groups, such as the "Big Fish, Small Pond" and "Country Squires" that might be found in an affluent, semirural suburb; or the "Bohemian Mix" and "Young Digerati" in New York's Tribeca neighborhood. Knowing the characteristics and tastes of these segments makes it possible to predict that the first two groups pick Lexus as a top car model, whereas the city clusters prefer a Mini Cooper or a Range Rover.

Conducting Original Research

Two relatively simple projects can enhance the implementation of your communications plan. The first is a media trend analysis that will give you data on media coverage of your organization and issues. The second involves taking stock of public opinion research to determine if you need to mobilize the people who already support you, win the support of those sitting on the fence, or raise overall awareness of your issue.

Media Trend Analysis

Effective communication with your prime audiences requires a thorough understanding of the quantity, quality, and character of the press coverage—news reporting and editorial commentary—that has gone before. It also demands detailed attention to aspects of reporting that are crucial to understanding how your issues or organization are perceived by the media, including the following:

Story placement. Is media coverage of your organization or set of issues usually considered hard news that might appear on the front page of a newspaper, the home page of a media Web site, or the lead story on a newscast? Or are you receiving feature coverage in the lifestyle sections of a newspaper, longer and softer segments on local television, or Web-based "News You Can Use" info-bits?

Tone. Are the stories dry renderings of events or exposés of scandals?

Bylines. Is the issue covered consistently by a senior reporter or haphazardly by a rotating roster of different bylines?

Messengers and spokespeople. Who is quoted or interviewed? Government officials, nonprofit leaders, or advocates?

Messages. How have the media portrayed your organization in the past? How do your spokespeople describe the issues? Does the coverage suggest actions that can be taken by volunteering, joining, or participating in some way?

The proliferation of electronic news databases has cut the time and cost involved in researching past coverage. If you are a part of a college, university, law firm, or larger organization with research capacity, your group may have a subscription to LexisNexis. This enables you to easily and effectively search tens of thousands of media outlets. Less costly searches can be done by subscribing to the *Wall Street Journal* online, with limited searches of that paper and the Dow Jones newswires. Free services are available with the *New York Times* online archive and Google News, in some cases going back more than a century.

In the case of an issue covered extensively by the media, the volume of available stories may be overwhelming, but you can narrow your search by using several specific key words or phrases. To yield even more precise results, subscriber services like LexisNexis allow users to limit the search to key words that appear prominently in a story, such as in the headline or first paragraph. Try searching only stories of five hundred words or more to eliminate articles with only a casual reference to the topic. If your focus is media in a specific city or state, going directly to a local media outlet Web site can be more efficient.

Once you have a good sample of media coverage, have one person review the stories by date, placement, tone, length, reporter, blogger interest, words and phrases used to describe your organization and the issues, names and titles of spokespeople, and so on. This information can, if necessary, be put into a simple database and analyzed in a variety of ways. But after reading even a dozen or more stories, you will find that trends appear.

Look for news hooks (that is, reasons for running the story) and seasonal or other patterns. Could your input have made it a better piece? Summarize your findings in a media analysis with recommendations for the future, and present it to your media planning group or board of directors to argue for greater investments in communications activities or to show the positive effects of your work. Plan to update the analysis every six to twelve months to help with planning and evaluation.

Quantitative and Qualitative Research

Public opinion research falls into two main categories. The most familiar kind is quantitative research, such as public opinion polls or surveys conducted among scientifically drawn samples of several hundred to several thousand people. The second is qualitative research, such as focus group discussions.

Public Opinion Polling

A public opinion poll of fifteen hundred to two thousand adults can estimate within a 3 to 5 percent error rate the number of people who agree or disagree with statements based on phone interviews or computer questionnaires.

"Top-line data" from the opinion poll show the overall result for each question. Below the top line are demographic breakdowns for each question, also known as the cross-tabulated data or just "cross tabs." For example, along with a top-line finding that more American households own dogs than cats, poll results might reveal regional or demographic data (for example, dog ownership is highest in Southern states) and cross-tabs that result from comparing answers to poll questions (for example, cat owners are more likely to own more than one pet, and there are more pet cats than dogs in the United States).

Original survey research can be costly. Local or state-based polling of five hundred to six hundred randomly chosen people can cost $20,000 to $40,000, depending on how many questions are asked. Prices for national polls of one thousand respondents start at $35,000 to $40,000. Fortunately, there are many ways to access existing polling data at a small fraction of that price, as we outline later in this chapter.

With a poll that is well designed and executed, you can

- Gather information needed for message development
- Measure public awareness of your organization, mission, and issue agenda
- Quantify people's level of support and reactions to test messages
- Identify target audiences

In addition to polling samples of your target audiences, conducting qualitative research is a highly effective way to understand how your target audiences think and feel about issues, and why. Let's look at some of the options.

Focus Groups

Typically, a focus group is a collection of twelve to twenty people selected according to certain characteristics for a two-hour, moderated discussion.

Focus groups can be used to uncover new themes that persuade people, to test reactions to specific language and messages, and to provide valuable feedback on visual presentations. Focus groups are often conducted prior to a public opinion survey to explore the range of attitudes people hold on an issue and to help test the wording of questions to be asked on a poll.

Focus groups also are conducted after a survey is completed. In this case, the purpose of the focus group is to use the richness of in-depth conversation to better understand the poll findings. For example, women between the ages of forty-four and sixty-five might be asked to explore the importance of retirement planning, whereas parents of young children would be asked to participate in groups on issues related to family policy and early education.

Unlike polls, focus groups explore the values, beliefs, and motivations underlying participants' opinions. Focus groups cost $8,000 to $10,000 for two sessions; you'll need at least four to understand how the issues being discussed are viewed among target audiences.

In-Depth Interviews (IDIs)

As the name implies, in-depth interviews, also called IDIs, focus on one or two people at a time. They are best for probing sensitive or confidential information that is hard to discuss in group settings, or for learning the opinions of people who are unlikely to attend a focus group.

Online Research

Considering that 71 percent of adults in the United States regularly use the Internet, virtual qualitative research has many advantages. It can give you a representative sample of hard-to-reach populations and allows for greater geographic dispersal of participants and higher response rates, as respondents can participate at their convenience. Online methods also lessen the opportunity for individuals to dominate or persuade others, and encourage honest dialogue.

Chat room format. This is essentially a virtual online version of a traditional focus group. Groups are held in real time over the Web with participants logging in and participating during a set time frame, generally an hour or two. A moderator logs in, and the group is conducted in the same way groups are conducted offline.

Bulletin board format. Here, a focus group is conducted over a four- or five-day period. Participants agree to log on to a Web site when it is most convenient for them, and to respond to questions from the moderator and the comments of other participants. Because of the longer time frame, this type of dialogue allows those who would not otherwise be able to participate to do so.

Instant-Response Dial Sessions

Dial sessions allow participants, using instant-response dial technology, to register their reactions to information presented to them. Republican pollster Frank Luntz calls these "people meters" and describes their many benefits in his book *Words That Work: It's Not What You Say, It's What People Hear.*

Dial sessions are generally made up of thirty to forty people, conducted classroom style and lasting two to three hours. Participants are given a wireless device with numbers from 1 (negative response) to 100 (positive response); they "dial in" their reactions to what is presented to them: videos, public service announcements, or live presentations. Virtually anything can be presented during a dial session. Reactions are captured instantaneously and displayed in a line that is superimposed over the tested material. Every time the line rises or falls, something significant has occurred and is evaluated by pollsters.

• • •

If you decide to conduct original research, make sure you find a researcher or pollster who will work with you and allow you to watch behind a two-way mirror or online so that you can have a front-row seat to the response.

Lower-Cost Alternatives to Original Research

Because public opinion research is so important in the framing of messages and targeting of specific audiences, it should be a component of every communications strategy. Unfortunately, as noted earlier, the cost of commissioning an original poll may be prohibitive. It may not be necessary to hire your own pollster, however. Thousands of polls are conducted each year, and numerous databases contain significant amounts of public opinion polling data on a wide range of issues. The news media, polling firms, foundations, and other large nonprofits often make their data available online for free or a modest fee.

Online Resources

Data on a wide range of issues can be obtained for free or at low cost from academic, private research, or organizational sponsors, including the news media. Two of the best resources are university-based archives: the Roper Center for Public Opinion Research at the University of Connecticut and the National Opinion Research Center (NORC) at the University of Chicago.

The Roper Center was founded in 1947 and today maintains the world's largest archive of survey data. Its mission statement says that "in selecting surveys for inclusion in its library, the Center insists on research of the highest professional quality . . . [with] a predominant interest in social and political information from national samples." The Center's archives hold more than five hundred thousand questions from 150 sources dating back to 1935, gleaned from surveys by Gallup, Roper, Harris Interactive, Yankelovich, the National Opinion Research Center, *ABC News*/the *Washington Post*, *NBC News*/the *Wall Street Journal*, the *Los Angeles Times*, Opinion Research Corporation, Field Research, *CBS News*/the *New York Times*, and many others. The Center charges a modest fee for its iPoll Databank services if you are purchasing a one-time search, usually no more than a few hundred dollars (http://ropercenter.uconn.edu). An annual subscription begins at $2,500, less for academic institutions.

The other leading source for opinion research data is NORC, a nonprofit corporation that conducts survey research in the public interest. Affiliated with the University of Chicago since 1946, NORC (http://norc.uchicago.edu) specializes in large-scale and national surveys and, since 1972, has conducted the General Social Survey (GSS), an ongoing assessment of attitudes among adults in U.S. households. The GSS archive includes answers from more than thirty-five thousand respondents to some twenty-nine hundred questions on topics ranging from national spending priorities and drinking behavior to marijuana use, race relations, and membership in voluntary associations.

A number of private resources for public opinion research are also online. They are especially useful to small organizations and agencies that need to monitor developments in current issues. One of the best is the Poll Track service offered on the Web site Cloakroom (http://cloakroom.com), which offers state-based and nationwide political polling information. You can access this site by purchasing the *Almanac of American Politics*, by Michael Barone and Richard Cohen (Washington DC: National Journal, 2008; $74.95) or subscribing to the *National Journal*.

Cloakroom is hardly alone in providing high-quality, timely information at a modest cost. The Internet is a treasure trove of free opinion data compiled by private companies for their corporate clients, as well as by nonprofit organizations. These include Public Agenda Online, a service designed primarily for journalists by the Public Agenda Foundation of New York; the Gallup Organization of Princeton, New Jersey, perhaps the best-known polling firm in the world; the Pew Research Center for the People and the Press, a Washington DC–based project of The Pew Charitable Trusts of Philadelphia, which regularly conducts a poll to gauge how closely the public is following current news stories; and Charlton Research Company of Walnut Creek, California, which conducts regular surveys nationally and in California. All of these organizations have their own Web sites, many with links to other research organizations.

Internet-Based Public Opinion Research

As it has with so much else, the Internet has changed the way public opinion research is conducted. Harris Interactive (formerly the Harris Survey) has developed an online survey methodology that queries millions of potential respondents who have been recruited online, by telephone, by mail, and in person. Individuals can opt in to a given survey and respond online to a self-administered poll using Harris's proprietary interviewing software. Results are weighted according to the standard demographic data and by the propensity of individuals in that demographic group to be online.

Omnibus Polls

What if you're involved in a cutting-edge issue that has not yet been researched by others? If you've checked existing archives and still come up empty-handed, you may want to do state or local-level polling to supplement the results of a national poll. If the cost of an original poll is too high, there are alternatives. One way is to get your questions included on one of the regular "omnibus surveys" conducted by larger private polling organizations.

The premise of an omnibus is simple. Several organizations each pose a handful of questions and share the costs. The surveys usually use large samples and ask the standard demographic questions about voting behavior, age, sex, race, income, education, and so forth that are the basis of targeting. Adding a single question to the Caravan, one of these national omnibus surveys of adults, can cost your group as little as $2,000. At this price, five to ten questions on an omnibus poll could give you answers at less than half the price of a specially commissioned poll. This service typically does not include more than cursory advice on question wording or any analysis of the results, and you will have to do your own interpretation. You will, however, receive demographic cross-tabulations on the answers to your questions.

• • •

Understanding where your target audiences stand on the issues is key to reaching them. The knowledge you will gain in surveying the public opinion landscape is a crucial element of any communications strategy. The resource section at the end of this book includes a listing of leading public opinion research databases and firms.

Chapter 4

Framing and Developing Messages

- Develop values-based messages.
- Understand your audiences' levels of thinking.
- Frame the debate and win on your issue or campaign.

BY TARGETING AUDIENCES, you are deciding what segments of the public you want to reach, and sometimes those you will ignore. By properly framing messages, you build a communications strategy on widely held values that shape opinions. And within those frames, you can create targeted messages, assembling the specific concepts and language that will resonate with those who are persuadable and ready to move to action.

Lori Dorfman, director of the Berkeley Media Studies Group, is an expert in framing messages related to public health, family, and a wide range of social policies. She describes the process this way: "Frames are mental structures that help people understand the world, based on particular cues from outside themselves that activate assumptions and values they hold within themselves."

Dorfman uses the following example to demonstrate the power of frames. She asks audiences, "What do you think is the text of the following phrase?"

ECONOMIC DEVELOPMENT

People's knowledge of the alphabet and language leads them to believe the words to be "ECONOMIC DEVELOPMENT." However, the next illustration reveals the hidden text.

FCQNQMIC DFVFIQRMFNT

The example of these figures shows that our brains are trained to respond to seemingly familiar information with a sort of "default" mode. If we are presented with new information, however, we go to a new frame. The challenge is to move people beyond their default mode if you are working to introduce a new frame or to reframe the words describing a set of ideas, themes, action steps, or policies. As you identify the groups that are most likely to share your goals, you think about the messages that will resonate most when talking to them, and develop winning frames that fit their existing beliefs and values.

Developing Values-Based Messages

Nearly all nonprofits have mission statements based on core values and principles. For some groups, these may be values related to care of one's family, personal liberty, integrity, equality, or fairness. Others may base their mission on values of improving education or promoting democracy, equal opportunity, or global health. Faith-based groups regularly blend their values of spirituality, equality, and honesty, with messages in sermons to their local congregations and in their missionary work overseas.

Pollsters and academics have been doing research and writing about the connections among values, framing, and communications for several decades. In 1993, the Brookings Institution published a book, *Values and Public Policy,* in which pollster Daniel Yankelovich examined how changes in the economy reshape American values. He examined a set of core American values that include freedom, equality before the law, equality of opportunity, fairness, achievement, patriotism, democracy, American exceptionalism, caring beyond self, religion, and luck. Yankelovich points out that "[a] focus on core values is not enough, however. It must be supplemented by a working understanding of how changing cultural values interact with the core values."

A few years later, in 1995, MIT Press published *Environmental Values in American Culture,* by Willett Kempton, James Boster, and Jennifer Hartley, making the case for and predicting renewed attention to global warming and other environmental changes, from an academic perspective. The authors explored in detail how beliefs and values together influence preferences for or against environmental policies. A decade later, the world is now focused on global warming and the potential impact for life on Earth; the elements of these current debates and proposals were outlined in a comprehensive review of public opinion, values, and belief systems examined in detail by the MIT Press authors. The impact of cultural activities, such as former vice president Al Gore's Oscar-winning documentary, *An Inconvenient Truth,* helped move the issues of climate change and the environment front and center on the agenda of mainstream media after nearly a decade of neglect.

For more than a decade, Nancy Belden, John Russonello, and Kate Stewart (of the polling and research firm Belden Russonello & Stewart, or BRS) have been tracing the impact of values on framing, messaging, and supporting the mission of nonprofits. They built on the work of Milton Rokeach, the late social psychologist and author of *The Nature of Human Values,* and Rushworth Kidder, a former senior columnist at the *Christian Science Monitor,* and examined more than forty years of public opinion data.

In a report done for CCMC and under the heading "Communicating Values," BRS points out that "before advocates can understand where public opinion is headed, they need to know from where it is derived." For this reason, it is important to understand the discussions around values as "those core beliefs that underlie all attitudes and behavior. Although attitudes will change, values usually endure across a person's life span, and only change slowly from generation to generation. Some values take precedence over others, as people organize their values into groups and arrange them hierarchically," according to BRS.

The BRS researchers identified eleven values considered fundamental to Americans' belief system and arranged them into two main categories (listed below): "Primary values prove dominant when competing with other values, while secondary ones are important but often vulnerable to other values." Thus messages based on primary values generally will trump those based on secondary values. This may explain why certain direct mail appeals, whether online or by mail, do better than others. Or why an op-ed essay gets chosen by the editor. Or why a person may join your organization over another.

Primary Values	**Secondary Values**
Responsibility to care for one's family	Responsibility to care for others
Responsibility to care for oneself	Personal fulfillment
Personal liberty	Respect for authority
Work	Love of country or culture
Spirituality	
Honesty and integrity	
Fairness and equality	

As you are developing messages for a collaborative initiative, fund-raising event, or issue campaign, or positioning your organization in the media, keep in mind that you should first identify the core values that may attract people to your cause. If values collide, and they often do, sort out which one trumps the other, under what circumstances, and why.

An example by BRS: "When Americans evaluate a criminal justice issue—drug laws, death penalty, mandatory minimum sentencing—they weight the conflicting responsibility they feel for the safety of their families with their desire for fairness toward others. In most cases, concerns over safety win, but there are times when the affront to fairness is so great that it outweighs all other values." An example would be the case of putting juveniles, especially those sixteen and under, in adult prisons due to over-crowded conditions.

Values-based messages can also bring mixed definitions, or what cognitive linguists call "contested concepts." In his book *Whose Freedom? The Battle over America's Most Important Idea,* linguist George Lakoff notes, "Important ideas like freedom that involve values and have a complex internal structure are usually contested—that is, different people have different understandings of what they mean."

Take the word *responsibility.* It may have one meaning to one group of people and another to others, depending on their backgrounds, education levels, personal experiences, family structure, and so on. In 2006, when voters were asked in a poll conducted by Harris Interactive for the Women Donors Network in its Moving Forward project, "When you hear the term *personal responsibility,* which of the following comes closest to what you believe? Sixty percent of voters picked: if you do something wrong you will accept the consequences of your action; while 29% said: is an opportunity to live up to your own potential, make sound decisions and ultimately improve lives and communities."

As Lakoff explains in *Whose Freedom?* "In general, contested concepts have uncontested cores—central meanings that almost everyone agrees on. The contested parts are left unspecified, blanks to be filled in by deep frames and metaphors." This is why it is so very important when you are communicating messages about a concept, organization, campaign, or issue that is new, unknown, or contested, that you fill in these unspecified blanks with frames and metaphors that people understand.

In the 1990s, the nonprofit FrameWorks Institute developed a multi-disciplinary, multimethod approach to communications called Strategic Frame Analysis™. This approach uses techniques from cognitive and social sciences to document the public's deeply held worldviews and widely held assumptions. It is strategic in the sense that it empirically tests for the impact of dominant frames on public reasoning and then develops and tests alternative re-frames that can be shown to improve understanding of and support for specific policies. Among the core tenets of this approach are the following observations:

- People are not blank slates.
- Communications are interactive and frame-based.
- Communications resonate with people's deeply held values and worldviews.
- People routinely default to the "pictures in their heads."
- People can be redirected to a different way of thinking if the composition and order of communications is changed.

To help people further understand how this approach can be used to communicate to audiences, FrameWorks explored framing elements at three "levels of thinking" based on research related to how human brains process information:

Level One. Big ideas and values: responsibility, personal liberty, fairness, family, equality, opportunity, safety, and other core values

Level Two. Issues and movements: women's, civil, and human rights; education and health care reform; children's issues; the environment; and more

Level Three. Specific policies or legislation, such as TANF, 4(e) entitlements, 150 account, pre-K, 0–8, HAVA, NVRA, TBA, minimum wage, MDGs, FOIA, and paid sick leave

You might find it helpful to think of values-based messages as a flower (see Figure 4.1). Most people buy cut flowers for their homes for sight and smell, or to delight their senses. Think of these people as at Level One (big ideas), wanting just to enjoy the flowers, but not really caring about their Latin names, how to cultivate them, or any of the details about how they get to the florist or are produced in world markets. Level One audiences are attracted to the broad concept of an idea or policy because it reflects their personal values. They are drawn less to detail than the people in the next two levels.

Level Two is the stems that bring the nutrients to the flowers. Level Two audiences are interested in more than just the Big Idea. They want to know more about the details that fuel it. For example, Level Two people might want to know how many varieties of a particular flower exist, or whether a

FIGURE 4.1

Big Ideas Get Attention

Too often messages are focused on the *roots* of a project, or on the *stems* related to issues and movements. It is the big ideas and values that resonate with **large** audiences. The challenge is to begin at the right level of thinking with your audience and start down a path that produces support for your organization, issues, ideas and policy proposals.

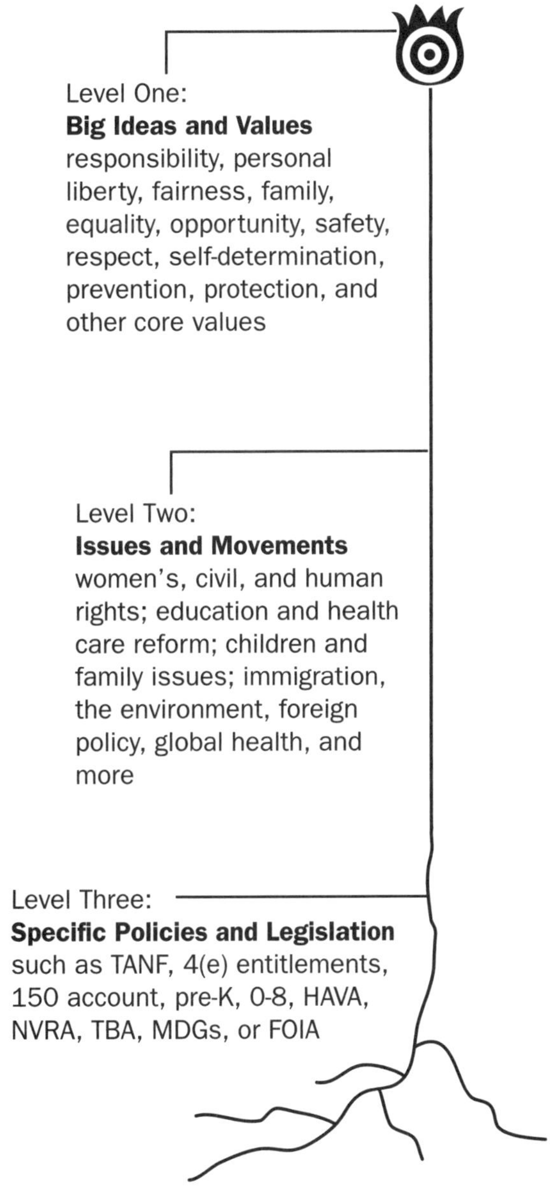

Level One:
Big Ideas and Values
responsibility, personal liberty, fairness, family, equality, opportunity, safety, respect, self-determination, prevention, protection, and other core values

Level Two:
Issues and Movements
women's, civil, and human rights; education and health care reform; children and family issues; immigration, the environment, foreign policy, global health, and more

Level Three:
Specific Policies and Legislation
such as TANF, 4(e) entitlements, 150 account, pre-K, 0-8, HAVA, NVRA, TBA, MDGs, or FOIA

Source: Belden Russonello & Stewart

certain flower is easy or difficult to grow. Level Two people are movement activists, advocates, or members of issue-oriented organizations.

Finally, there are the roots, the dirt, the nutrients—and sometimes the weeds—where the flowers germinate. It takes an intense level of expertise and training in horticulture to grow flowers. The "growers" at Level Three are the experts who probably use a lot of Latin terms to describe their flowers. They may compete in orchid shows or focus exclusively on perennials or greenhouse annuals. Basically, Level Three audiences are made up of individuals who are experts in their field.

When developing and communicating messages, it is important to understand that experts and advocates too often operate at a level different from that of their target audiences. The public is generally at Level One—looking for a conversation about values or beliefs before they can decide about supporting a group or cause, taking action, or sending money. People want to know if there is a personal "values connection" to your membership group or online network.

So ask: Can your conversation be opened at Level One? How best can you frame messages so as to increase awareness, concern, or saliency and move people to action?

In contrast, if you plan to communicate with leading experts or academics, you need to operate at their level of thinking. Craft your messages by including the language your audience uses. Make sure your conversation is at the right level, with a focus on one or two, but no more than three, key ideas or message points.

Values-Based Messages: Heard and Understood or Glazed Over?

Storytelling has become the norm for most mass media. Reporters say, "I need to put a face on the facts for my readers or viewers." Successful stories reflect core values and widely held beliefs in order to connect with the majority of your target audiences. But there is a challenge with storytelling. If the focus is on an individual, the audience may conclude that it is a personal problem without a broader public solution. And if the problem seems too overwhelming for them to help solve, their eyes glaze over.

The bottom line is that messages are heard and acted on when the issues or organizations are relevant to the target audience. Convincing research shows that messages based on core American values are more potent and more likely to be received. For example, in nearly every focus group conducted about U.S. aid to poor or developing countries, someone in the

FIGURE 4.2

Ranking of Most Important Issues

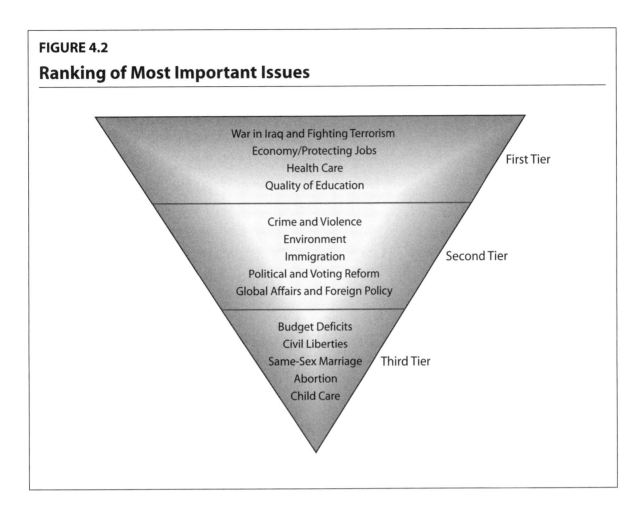

group says, "It is better to 'teach a man to fish than give him a fish.'" Thus a message of self-sufficiency will be heard over one of entitlement.

You need to speak in a language the target audience understands and play to the strengths you may have, as expressed in public opinion. If the economy is a top issue of concern, then weave into your messages how your group helps strengthen the economy. If you are working on child welfare or vulnerable youth, speak to the issues of safety or education; both are consistently top concerns as expressed in public opinion polls.

Since 2006, opinion polls have generally shown that the public considers the war in Iraq, the economy, and health care to be the top issues facing the United States. Figure 4.2 is based on a compilation of survey results over the past several years. For example, the issue of the budget deficit does not represent a top concern for most people. When people hear these words they tend to think of a government process not necessarily connected to their lives. The concept of budget deficit reframed in terms of cuts in programs and services raises concerns about job security, loss of income, and other economic issues that affect people's livelihood. Thus reframed, the budget deficit moves into the top tier of concerns related to the economy where a majority of the public and media will listen and be supportive.

Keep in mind that public opinion can be shaped over time by repeated messages in the news and entertainment media. But public opinion does not take its shape only from news coverage. Most people also rely on the viewpoints of trusted acquaintances to help them form opinions on an unfamiliar topic. Those with the greatest influence are the familiar faces and trusted voices of those closest to us—as shown in the innermost circle of communications effectiveness (Figure 4.3), discussed in the next section. We may receive a thousand messages on a topic over television and ten from our relatives, but the two sources can be roughly in balance, because communications that come from personally trusted sources are usually more effective.

FIGURE 4.3

Circles of Communications Effectiveness

Mass media: radio, TV, cable, satellites, and movies
Newspapers, direct mail, and Internet
Clergy, doctors, and counselors
Close friends and associates
Extended family
Nuclear family
Individual

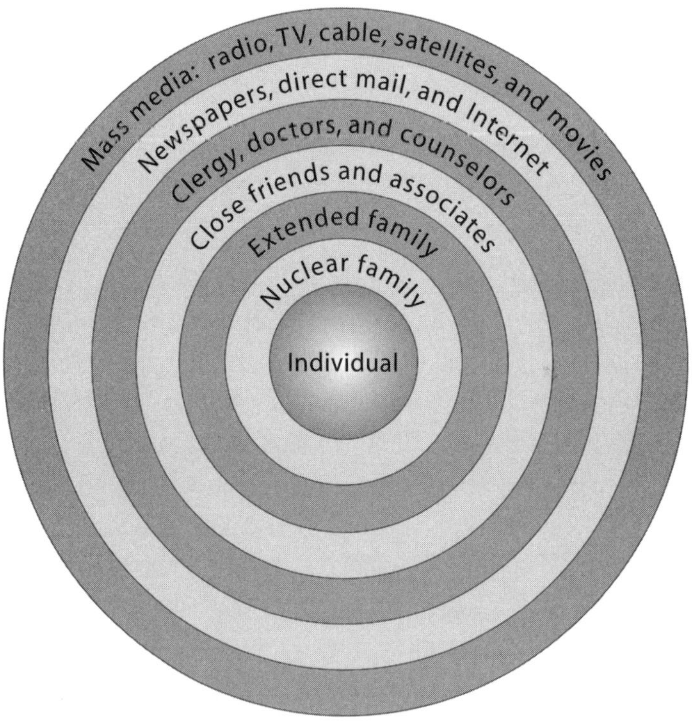

Source: Vincent J. Breglio

The Circles of Communications Effectiveness

The circles of communications effectiveness model was developed by Vince Breglio, a leading Republican research analyst and public opinion expert on a range of issues that include the economy, the environment, international affairs, education, family policy, and women's voting patterns; he has conducted thousands of focus groups and public opinion polls over the past thirty years. His model (Figure 4.3) illustrates the different ways people initially hear about ideas and issues and where they go to validate or refute new information.

At the center of trusted sources of information is the nuclear and extended family. The main source of ideas, words, and phrases for dealing with a wide range of issues is one's personal circle of family members. As one female focus group member from Baltimore told Breglio, "The only thing I know is what my father told me about. I've seen it in the media, but I never knew that much about it until he started talking about it." Beyond the family, voters turn to friends and other influential people, such as clergy and caring professionals, for information. Again and again, when people are asked whose word means the most to them, their responses are short and to the point: "my doctor," "my minister [rabbi]," or "my mother or father."

The media can help shape the attitudes of someone who has had no direct experience with a person or an issue. However, the average person will look back to an inner circle of family and friends to sort out conflicting information to reinforce his or her beliefs. Thus, if your messages and action steps relate to personal experiences and to values that can be reinforced by family and close friends, you can build and mobilize support more quickly and effectively. If you are asking people to form an opinion on a topic with which they have had little or no direct experience, you must first engage in a public education effort that ties your message into their existing personal values and beliefs. See the resources section for a list of excellent books, Web sites, and other resources related to values-based messaging.

Developing Winning Frames and Effective Messages

Why do environmentalists usually talk about "energy efficiency" instead of "energy conservation," and describe weather conditions as "climate change" instead of the "greenhouse effect"? Why do family policy advocates describe family leave as a "minimum standard" instead of a "government mandate"? Why do civil rights advocates use the words "equal opportunity" and not "quotas"?

Survey research and focus groups conducted by environmentalists showed that the interchangeable words "energy efficiency" and "conservation" had two completely different meanings to the general public and policymakers. According to their findings, the word "conservation" was associated with lifestyle sacrifices, such as turning down the heat and wearing a sweater. In contrast, "energy efficiency" seemed to indicate the positive uses of new technology to achieve reductions in energy use—doing more with less. The term "greenhouse effect" seemed benign to most people, evoking images of a greenhouse nurturing plants and flowers, not a threat to the earth as the alternative terms "climate change," "climate crisis," and "global warming" might suggest, especially as people personally experience wild changes in their local weather.

Family issues advocates found through research that family leave described or characterized as a "government mandate" provoked images of government control and straitjacketing employers. But characterizing family leave as a "minimum standard" just like the minimum wage or health and safety standards garnered more support.

Finally, when dealing with affirmative action programs, civil rights activists frequently use the term "equal opportunity," not "quotas." "Equal opportunity," according to the research, evokes images of a level playing field for all Americans. In contrast, the term "quotas" seems to many people like a strict, numbers-only system of favoring one group over another to foster equality.

The language, symbols, anecdotes, and other information used in a communications strategy are critical factors in determining whether it will succeed or fail. So developing effective messages that are framed to win is an important first step in any communications effort.

A Simple Way of Developing Messages

One of the very best tools to help develop messages and keep spokespeople "on message" is a chart called a message box (Figure 4.4), a system developed by messaging expert Michael Sheehan. At the center is the basic or core message—the one-liner stating your overarching goal that you use if there is no time for anything else. Your core message should be a simple declarative sentence that is short and memorable. The average sound bite on radio and television is less than ten seconds long and shrinking. Even in newspaper articles, the trend is toward shorter quotes. One of the top expert media trainers, Sheehan regularly develops message boxes for top government officials and heads of large nonprofits and corporations.

FIGURE 4.4

Sample Message Box

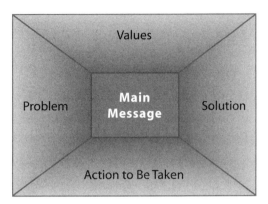

Source: *Michael Sheehan Associates, Inc.*

You should state the goal of your policy, project, research, or initiative as a central theme. Then start with a value that embodies the media effort. The other panels contain a statement summarizing the problem, the solution to the problem, and an action the target audience can take. In the course of an interview, a spokesperson can start from the central point, then move back and forth from the problem, the solution, and the action, depending on how the conversation flows. The desired effect is to make the same points repeatedly, but in a natural way that does not seem like rote repetition.

Creative Brainstorming

In the 1960s and 1970s, a group of government officials came up with the names for important federal agencies and programs by simply discussing appropriate and powerful words. The names given to the Peace Corps, Head Start, the Equal Employment Opportunity Commission, and the Environmental Protection Agency were the result of informal discussions, without the benefit of extensive branding research. In one case, the words "equal opportunity" were framed into the commission's name. In another case, government officials wanted to be careful to indicate that their agency would "protect" the environment. The lesson here is that a group of informed individual experts can develop winning frames by just talking about a particular issue.

In a small brainstorming session, creative and committed people armed with opinion research can come together to discuss winning frames and messages. Sometimes brilliant ideas take only a few hours to develop. Other times, the process can get bogged down with too many "cooks." But in order to develop an effective communications strategy, take the time to develop messages that are values based, understood and supported by your target audiences, and suitable for being put into short ten- to twenty-second sound bites for use with media.

Case Study: Messages for Expanding Early Education

For years, advocates of expanding pre-kindergarten (pre-K) education commonly referred to the services they were trying to expand through additional government resources as "day care" and "child care." Focus groups and polling showed that these two terms equated in the public's mind to "babysitting."

The original frame used by both the media and the advocacy community was disempowering in the public's mind. Therefore, advocates began searching for another set of terms to frame their issue. Based on their research, terms like "early care and education," "early learning," and "early childhood development" replaced "day care" and "child care" in the policy debate. That's because the research found that the most powerful frames on this issue linked pre-K to school readiness and better performance in the early grades—a focus on the educational needs of children, not the babysitting needs of their parents.

As the early care and education community began using these new terms among target audiences and with the media, the public dialogue on the issue began to change, although the process did take several years. Such words as "quality," "accessible," and "affordable" are key framing concepts that maintained support among parents and other audiences. (In Chapter Nine, we revisit the topic of early education with a case study on the importance of selecting the right messenger.)

Chapter 5

Navigating a Changing Industry

- Anticipate the needs of multiplatform journalism.
- Plan to make your Web site a TV station.
- Use media trends to shape outreach.

IN 2006, WHEN Illinois senator Barack Obama announced his "roots" trip to Africa, Lynn Sweet, the Washington bureau chief of the *Chicago Sun-Times,* pitched her editors for the assignment to cover this historic trip through several countries. Nearly all major Illinois media were planning to join the senator and his family at a time when issues facing sub-Saharan Africa were making front-page news: the spread of HIV/AIDS, natural disasters, climate change, food and water shortages, and ruinous civil wars.

Most Chicago media were sending teams that included photographers, camera crews, sound technicians, correspondents, and working journalists. The cost for a space on the media plane was in the tens of thousands of dollars for each person. After doing a budget reality check, Sweet and top editors decided to try something different. A few days before Sweet was to leave for Africa, a MacBook computer arrived in her office along with a small Canon digital still camera, a Sony digital video cam, and a digital audio recorder. She had a few days of long-distance learning from the IT editor in Chicago and was off—solo—with the equipment in her backpack and vest.

For the next few weeks, Sweet filed her regular news stories and column by wireless, DSL, and dial-up connections. In addition, she wrote a blog, participated in online chat rooms with readers, took photographs that appeared on the front page of the paper and on the home page of the *Sun-Times* Web site, conducted audio interviews with dozens of newsmakers, and produced top-quality video files that were edited and posted online. The *Sun-Times* did a special promotion of her trip and sent readers to the Web site for complete coverage. Readers responded enthusiastically.

"One reader sent an e-mail about her daughter being a student in Kenya. She met me at the airport when we landed in Nairobi and I was able to work in a local story from the beginning of our coverage. I got very little sleep, but was often beating out my competition," Sweet told a group of reporters at the Journalism and Women Symposium session that year.

What was a unique experience for a traditional print reporter in 2006 is becoming standard for many journalists around the world. Journalists are now "news gatherers" for "multiplatform" digital media created by the convergence of newspapers, magazines, television, video, photography, cable, phones (both land lines and cell), audio, and the Internet. The *Washington Post* now calls itself an education company, and Google is fast becoming mass media. This chapter is a mere snapshot of a moving picture soon to be on permanent fast-forward.

These trends underscore how important it is for you to cultivate personal relationships with professional and citizen journalists, both on the Web and in person. In addition, your organization needs to decide on the role it wants to play: Will you be a content provider or an influencer of others who provide content, or both?

Lynn Sweet's "backpack journalism" is a modern approach to addressing the news industry's decades-long need to grapple with evolving technologies. In the 1950s, the arrival of television and its evening newscasts helped bring on the decline of afternoon newspapers. In the 1960s and 1970s, the higher-quality sound of FM radio led many AM stations to change their formats from music to news and talk. In the 1980s, cable news offered the first challenge to the video news supremacy of the major broadcast networks, even as it struggled to fill twenty-four hours of programming a day.

Back then, a communications team adept at navigating long-term trends would have cultivated more relationships at the morning newspaper, or developed a roster of spokespeople to appear as guests on radio and cable programs. These changes were significant, but they unfolded over a long period of time, and were relatively gradual compared to the current pace of change in the news industry.

Today, all previous forms of journalism are up for grabs; the revolutionary technology of the Internet has made it possible for a single person with a unique story, an interesting opinion, or even a funky video to reach a global audience. The challenges the Internet poses to the news business are unprecedented, because it has fractured the *fundamentals* of news consumption, and in ways that are constantly and rapidly evolving.

In response, there is an overall trend in the mainstream media to cut costs, either by giving more assignments and duties to the reporters who remain on staff or by relying more on freelancers to report, edit, and produce news content. The trend is most noticeable at the big television news networks, which have closed many previously well-staffed bureaus, leaving a single full-time freelancer in place to handle routine developments and provide support when highly paid correspondents and anchors "parachute" into town for a major event. Local freelancers shoot much of the television footage we see from overseas, with the closest network correspondent providing voice-over narration. This practice is also becoming common in bureaus based in the United States.

The trend is spreading to other media, complicating communications work for nonprofits because freelancers move around or work many different kinds of stories, blurring or eradicating the traditional beat system.

Spectrum Auctions

Starting in 2009, federal law will require all full-power television stations to broadcast only in digital format. This won't affect cable subscribers, but those with older television sets using "rabbit ears" or other standard antennas to capture television over the air will need to purchase converters or new television sets.

Far more important, the change will mean that television stations can compress their signals into a smaller part of the broadcast spectrum than they are now allotted. Much of the remaining spectrum will be auctioned to companies interested in setting up wireless high-speed data services that can reach as far as a TV signal can and even go through buildings.

Compare that potential to the free limited wireless services currently offered by hotels, municipalities, and the like, and you begin to understand how using the newly available spectrum for wireless networks could translate into far more affordable high-speed Internet delivery for more organizations and individuals, enabling nonprofit organizations to become important direct providers of high-quality video and audio programming from their Web sites.

The Impact of the Internet

Unlike previous ways of communicating, the Internet doesn't just inform people; it empowers them. As the Project for Excellence in Journalism (PEJ), an initiative of The Pew Charitable Trusts, points out in its 2007 annual report, *The State of the News Media,* "Technology is redefining the role of the citizen—endowing the individual with more responsibility and command over how he or she consumes information—and that new role is only beginning to be understood." It has dethroned the previous model of "one-to-many" communications in favor of a "many-to-many" model. (Pew also produces a biennial survey of U.S. media consumption habits, cited later in this chapter.) A compelling example of how this new role might play out in the future took place in early 2007 in the aftermath of the shootings at Virginia Tech in Blacksburg, Virginia. A video taken by a student on his cell phone included the sound of gunshots outside Norris Hall, where thirty-one people died. CNN ran it repeatedly. The first reports of the shooting and consequent updates were carried on the school's Web site, which immediately became a key resource for the public and media alike. The *New York Times* linked to a student's Facebook page that had information about who was safe and who was missing, short-circuiting the usual progression of a news story through the editorial filter. A new form of storytelling emerged in this tragedy, blurring the lines that once separated journalism from the subjects it covered.

A related change, and one of great potency for the nonprofit community, is the rise in the number and popularity of highly opinionated, often activist commentators whose work appears only on Web sites. Their regular posting on Web logs gives us the term "blog." This community, also known as the "blogosphere," derives its mission and identity in large part from its opposition to the traditional or "mainstream" media.

To make the point clear, some bloggers have adopted the mantle of "citizen journalist" and are taken seriously by major mainstream media, changing the business of news in every traditional medium.

The Pew Internet Project pointed out a behavioral trait of broadband users that may prove just as important to the Internet's future: they are far more likely than dial-up users to create or post content to the Internet.

The rapid diffusion of broadband has reached the tipping point, and most households now use fast DSL or wireless connections. People now surf at lightning speed, move from site to site, download audio and video, and post any content, even video, easily and for free. Inexpensive digital cameras have proliferated, and suddenly anyone can be a television producer. Expectations for the Internet have changed dramatically, as more people study, shop, or socialize online.

The future of the Internet remains hard to chart because it represents such a radical transformation in the relationships between individuals and the information that shapes their lives. But two points are clear: first, the Internet is affecting the daily work of journalism in ways that are crucial to the success of any communications strategy. Whoever you are and whatever your cause, you need to understand these changes. Second, the low cost of communications over the Internet makes it especially valuable to groups with limited resources; your Web site could become a television or radio station available around the world.

These developments, dramatic enough on their own, came on top of other important trends, including declining network television audiences and daily newspaper circulation, consolidation of ownership, staff cutbacks, and other attempts by the old media to adapt to the new environment. One longstanding trend that is accelerating as a result of technology and economic pressure finds more reporters working across platforms. A newspaper columnist may contribute additional text and a daily podcast to the paper's Web site; television news anchors write blogs; bloggers look for audio and video supplements for their text and links.

Years ago, a good communications strategy around an event or report might have included having an expert conduct a phone interview with a newspaper reporter; providing a television correspondent with video from a press conference, with background footage on the issue at hand; and booking your group's main spokesperson on a radio talk show. Increasingly, adapting to journalists' changing needs means moving outside traditional lines and offering all of these to everybody. The basic tools for media outreach remain the same in key ways, but the long-term trend is to combine them in a single package for all media.

A Revolution in the News Business

Television, radio, cable, and magazines are all generally in the same situation: protracted decline. They are responding in myriad ways. *Time* magazine has moved its publication date from Monday to the previous Friday, breaking with more than a half-century of tradition to stay relevant. The number of printed pages in weekly newsmagazines declines each year. One veteran *Newsweek* reporter whispered, "I think our editors see the magazine as a brochure for the Web site."

Network news organizations send their anchors, who in the past rarely left Manhattan, on a worldwide quest for ratings. Local television is shifting and expanding its schedules and can also be seen traveling the world for local stories, while national radio and television talk shows seek out reliably provocative guests who can talk in sound bites, rather than people who can share real expertise in an expanded vocabulary.

Local News Web Sites

Newspapers and local television stations around the country are moving in the same direction by paying greater attention to their Web sites. They are all trying to transform themselves into centers for community information, input, and involvement, offering message boards and chat rooms on many sites.

Most major daily newspapers, including the *Washington Post*, schedule regular Internet chats with key staff or authors of featured articles, who answer questions e-mailed by readers. The *Seattle Post-Intelligencer* has a virtual editorial board; readers can contribute thoughts, data, or commentary to shape editorials while they are being prepared for the next day's newspapers. The *Asheville* (NC) *Citizen-Times* posts articles by an array of community columnists.

The walls that separate news outlets from their audiences are growing more porous, if not crumbling entirely—and multiplying the opportunities for nonprofits to insert their viewpoints.

Wire Services

The importance of wire services can only grow as newspapers and broadcasters cut back on personnel and bureaus in the United States and abroad. And in 2008, one leading wire service added twenty-two entertainment reporters while cutting back on several news beats. Many a busy news editor has turned down a nonprofit's pitch for an exclusive interview, saying, "We'll just run the wire copy." Building a good relationship with your local wire service is therefore critical.

The Associated Press is the largest news agency in the world and is itself an American nonprofit organization, founded in 1846 by New York newspapers to avoid the duplicative costs of sending several rowboats out into the harbor to get news from ships arriving from Europe. Today its members include all major U.S. newspapers and radio and television broadcasters. Members allow AP to use their news items without prior clearance and pay a subscription fee to use AP content.

The AP is crucial to media relations for its ability to shape news coverage, even down to the choice of words. Its style manual is widely used and admired for its insistence on clear if somewhat flat prose. And AP bureaus carry a daybook or calendar of upcoming events, which is closely followed by other media. In most places, being listed on the AP daybook is a key to the success of any media outreach plan that includes conference calls, news conferences, and the like.

Reuters is a British-owned company with a focus on financial and market news, although in Washington DC and other capitals, it also reports on nonprofit lobbies, coalitions, and advocacy groups. The same is true of its rival **Bloomberg News.** Both companies make most of their profits providing data directly to the financial industry.

United Press International (UPI) was for decades the AP's chief rival, but had seven owners from 1992 to 2000, when the Unification Church purchased it, and its size and influence has declined sharply.

Pacific News Service (PNS) is a news wire service that focuses its coverage on ethnic minorities, youth, the elderly, immigrants, and others who are too frequently overlooked by mainstream media. PNS feeds news to subscribing mainstream and community newspapers through the AP Newswire. Founded in 1969 as an alternative source for news about the Vietnam War, it created **New America Media (NAM),** a California-based collaboration of ethnic news organizations, in 1996.

The National Newspaper Publishers News Service is operated by the National Newspaper Publishers Association (http://news.nnpa.org), also known as the Black Press of America. Founded during World War II, it distributes news, features, and commentary to two hundred member papers.

Women's eNews distributes stories of particular concern to women at womensenews.com. An online-only free subscription service, it covers religion, economics, health, science, sports, and politics, but with the women's perspective that is usually missing from mainstream media coverage. The news service distributes articles daily to its subscribers in the United States and abroad. Taking advantage of an emerging trend, Women's eNews uses freelance writers and recently retired reporters from around the world.

Daily Newspapers—Declining Circulation, but Still the Medium of Influential Elites

Although competition from television, cable, and the Internet has eroded some of their influence, newspapers, on paper and online, still remain a powerful force and an important source of news and opinion for influential segments of society. Their size and scope allow deeper coverage and analysis of a wide range of issues, compared to television and radio. Their influence on other news media also remains strong, and that fact is crucial to any communications strategy.

Politicians and policymakers pay close attention to the official editorial positions taken by the newspaper, and to the opinions expressed by regular columnists and even letters to the editor. Thus, placing an op-ed piece can be a springboard to interviews on television and radio.

Who is reading the daily papers these days, and how can you get your news and views in front of them? Go to the PEJ Web site, http://journalism.org. On an average day in 2006, 124 million people in America "read a newspaper," although fewer than half—fifty-one million—actually purchased one. The Pew Research Center survey found that 43 percent of respondents reported reading either the printed paper or the online version of their local paper the day before. But ten years earlier, fully half of respondents said they had read the print edition of their newspaper the day before. Although there have been gains in online newspaper readership, they have been outweighed by this overall decline.

Circulation has been declining in absolute terms since roughly 1990, and as a percentage of households since the 1920s, but the total number of daily papers has not changed much since the 1990s: it declined to 1,452 in 2006, just five less than the previous year. But fewer people run them, PEJ reports, with some three thousand fewer full-time newsroom staff in 2006 than at the industry's peak of 56,400 in 2000. Cuts tend to be deepest at the big-city newspapers, in part because so many smaller papers have already trimmed to the bone.

Of course, every newspaper in the land now has some kind of presence on the Web. Many sites also carry content and features like blogs and video that go far beyond what arrives on doorsteps each morning. Your communications strategy needs to adapt.

Newspapers vary greatly in the way they have developed their Internet editions. Most use content written for the print versions verbatim. Others provide only highlights, to lure readers to the newspaper. Pay attention to your newspaper's Web site. Does the site provide links to the Web sites of relevant nonprofit organizations? If a story is being published about your organization or issue, ask the reporter to include a link back to your Web site.

Ethnic Media

Solid growth in the audience for ethnic news media mirrors the increase of the U.S. ethnic population, which now hovers around sixty-four million people.

Part of the appeal of the ethnic press is its unique content. Ethnic papers cover neighborhood news and international developments of interest to their specialized audiences to a far greater extent than their mainstream counterparts. Updates on immigration law, where to find English classes, and how to get children immunized and enrolled in school offer practical information that the nation's newcomers are less likely to find in mainstream media.

For the most part, ethnic media in the twenty-first century follow the tradition of advocacy established in the 1800s when *Freedom's Journal*, the first black newspaper, was founded to counter negative commentary on black people. Ethnic media are usually not reluctant to take a stand on issues that affect their communities, and often partner and even crusade with advocates to help create change. The willingness of ethnic media to serve as the voices of their communities makes them excellent vehicles for community organizers.

Weekly Newspapers

Two important targets for nonprofit communications are big-city alternative weeklies, often with large African American constituencies, and traditional hometown weeklies that attract suburban and rural readers. As daily newspapers are losing readers overall, weeklies are generally thriving. Nearly eight hundred weekly papers are big enough to support Web sites, which can be accessed through a single source, www.weeklynewspapers.com/reviews.html.

These newspapers tend to focus on local events, personalities, and issues and are closely read, in part because they sit on coffee tables for a week or more and are sold or given away at stores and outlets in their target towns. Many have editorial pages featuring local editorials and op-eds, which makes them even better targets for outreach on local and regional issues than papers that run only news and features.

Television News—Adapting to Retain Audiences

Local television newscasts remain an important source of news for 53 percent of respondents in the 2006 Pew survey. That was a significant dip from 2004, when 59 percent said they were regular watchers of their local television news. Barring unforeseen developments, the downward trend is likely to continue. Pew's PEJ (http://journalism.org) regularly tracks these and other trends for television, including declining audiences for network newscasts and late-night news shows. It is also clear that the audience for network news is an aging one.

Of course, any nonprofit that places its key spokesperson in a good story on network news has still made a significant accomplishment. But in terms of impact and using audience as the metric, the value of such an appearance is only a fraction of what it was twenty-five years ago.

What to Do When Comedy Central Calls

If a book or op-ed your CEO has written gets good coverage, or your issue pops into the headlines, you may get a call from one of the main sources of news and information for large segments of the population: Comedy Central's fake news shows.

The Daily Show with Jon Stewart plays its comedy fairly straight, with Stewart as himself in the chair of his own talk show. (Stewart's "correspondents," however, often adopt fringe personas.) On *The Colbert Report*, host Steven Colbert plays the role of an opinionated conservative cable commentator. But they are similar shows in the sense that an appearance on either will reach a huge and sophisticated audience that includes young people who get no other news, and many not-so-young people besides.

The greatest risk to accepting an invitation to appear on either program is that the guest might not understand its premise, which is that the "news" is such a joke these days that it belongs on a comedy channel. The best way to figure out how to be a guest is to watch others do it: one national nonprofit executive prepared for an appearance by watching seven recent episodes with a media staffer present to comment on and "deconstruct" the interview segments.

Producers on these programs tell their guests not to try to be funny—straining too hard to "fit in" is almost as bad as not getting the joke in the first place. But one can learn to improve over time. In an initial appearance, one prominent Washington figure seemed shaken and taken aback when Stewart suggested that perhaps not only political collusion was going on in Washington but a fair amount of extramarital shenanigans to boot. On an appearance one year later, that same figure let similar outrageous statements go with a grin, like water off a duck's back.

Magazines—Adapting in Different Ways

Like the daily newspapers, the three big newsweeklies face a challenge from Internet news, and they appear to be adapting in several ways. One approach is to offer articles and features on the Web that are not found in the print version, and another is to offer more opinion, commentary, and analysis.

The circulation of the three big newsweeklies has been flat in recent years. In 2008, *Time* had a circulation of 4 million readers; *Newsweek*, 3.3 million; and *U.S. News & World Report*, 2 million. Getting a story or quote placed in any of these publications is still a major accomplishment, but one whose value is less today than in the past.

One notable trend is the rise in audience for niche weeklies like the *Week*, the *Economist*, and the *New Yorker*, which along with opinion magazines like the *Nation* and *National Review* are holding their own or growing.

Radio—the Convergence of Audio Platforms

Because they require less bandwidth to transmit, audio platforms started converging sooner than TV outlets did, and have progressed further. The use of iPods, MP3 players, digital HD radio, Internet streaming, and cell phones as music-listening devices keeps expanding, and new car radios come with an optional subscription satellite service offering hundreds of specialized channels. C-SPAN radio has taken full advantage of low-power stations in select communities. And community radio stations, like weekly newspapers, are thriving in many places as they expand audiences on their Web sites beyond broadcast range.

Many stations also post talk shows on the Web, to which you can direct members if they feature your issues or spokespeople.

Cable Television—Reaching Maturity and Looking for Opinions over News

The audience for the big cable news channels is also in decline, in part because of the increase in channel numbers. Although the cable news business continues to thrive financially, its future may lie with highly opinionated anchors like Keith Olbermann, Greta Van Susteren, Tavis Smiley, Lou Dobbs, and Bill O'Reilly. As the PEJ report notes, "The shifts toward even edgier opinion are also probably a response to another change. Cable is beginning to lose its claim as the primary destination for what was once its main appeal: news on demand. That is something the Internet can now provide more efficiently."

Bloggers—Eliminating the Gatekeepers

Essayists and pamphleteers have been around for centuries, but bloggers have no pre-Internet analog. They use search engines to troll the Web for news articles, simple software for easy posting, and high-speed connections to transfer video clips.

Bloggers make great use of the Internet's interactive ability, and can ask their readers for help with research. They can update entries instantly, and invite instant responses from third parties as part of an ongoing group commentary or dialogue. For anyone who wants to influence the public debate, the role of bloggers will only grow for this reason: they can bring a story to prominence without the blessing of mainstream media gatekeepers.

How a Blog Item Becomes a News Story

The breadth of interest the item might evoke determines whether news goes into a blog or into the paper. Blogs are designed to speak to an impassioned audience with a self-selected interest in a specific subject, be it mergers and acquisitions, baseball, cars or whatever. The newspaper is designed to appeal to a broader public, whose interests aren't necessarily pre-determined. One form delivers information that the readers know they're interested in. The other delivers information that should have broader import and can be serendipitous: here's something you didn't know you'd be interested in knowing.

What gives blogging its authenticity and momentum—its open access—also makes it vulnerable to manipulation. Yet some of the most popular bloggers are now forming businesses or associations with ethics codes, standards of conduct, and more. The paradox of professionalizing the medium to preserve its integrity as an independent citizen platform is the start of a complicated new era in the evolution of the blogosphere.

Source: John Geddes, managing editor, the *New York Times,* "Talk to the Newsroom" Web chat, Jan. 14, 2008

What Makes Blogs Different

Kevin Drum, who writes the "Political Animal" blog for *Washington Monthly*'s Web site, has a checklist of the distinguishing characteristics of blogs, first posted on May 11, 2004:

- The first-person style of blog posts often allows bloggers to do a better job of explaining complex subjects.... Newspaper articles, by contrast, are often so laden down by superfluous quotes and faux objectivity that by the time you're finished you're still confused about what's really going on.

- Blogs can aggregate information from a lot of different sources. The conventions of mainstream journalism don't really allow this.

- Blog posts can be any length. If a thought only deserves a couple of sentences, that's what it gets. If it deserves a thousand words, it can get that too.

- Bloggers don't have sources. That means there's very little original reporting in blogs, but it also means bloggers don't have to worry about protecting sources either.

- Blogs don't have to maintain the same standards as mainstream journalists. They can toss out ideas and rumors in a way that's genuinely valuable but hard to do in the mainstream media.

- Blogs allow unapologetic passion. Even on the op-ed page, convention dictates a sober, clinical style.

- Blogs can obsess over a single topic in a way that's hard for newspapers. This is sometimes a great weakness, of course, but it can also be a great strength at times.

- Finally, blogging is a two-way street. Blogs respond to each other and commenters respond to blogs. Blogs are a great way to get a quick read on what topics are really raising the blood pressure of that small group of people who care passionately about politics.

- Bottom line: blogs are different, not better or worse than radio, television or print, and the best blogs are the ones that truly take advantage of the unique strengths of the medium. Those that do, regardless of whether or not they're really 'journalism,' are genuinely new and powerful contributions to the political reporting scene.

Chapter 6

Making the Most of Your Resources

- Identify critical resources before you start, and allocate them carefully.
- Supplement in-house people power with talent drawn from internship, retiree, and executive loan programs.
- Manage your team's time wisely. Advance planning is key.
- Evaluate what worked; celebrate success.

Marshal Your Resources

Even the most seasoned media strategists are not magicians. They cannot wave a magic wand and produce good media coverage out of thin air. Your organization will need resources—people, time, money, and some basic tools—to set up and run a communications and media outreach office. Money is needed for graphics, databases, press lists, printing, postage, and other direct costs. As noted in Chapter One, the more money and resources you devote to communications strategies and press relations, the more media coverage your group will receive. However, with good leadership and the right commitment, even a volunteer team operating on a minimum budget can achieve good media coverage.

It is considerably easier for nonprofit organizations to raise money for strategic communications today than it was in the 1990s. At that time, grantmakers were accustomed to funding public education activities, such as reports, conferences, or public speaking events. However, the integrated approach inherent in strategic communications was a new concept. Non-profit communicators spent years persuading grantmakers that strategic communications ought to be a grantmaking priority. The situation now is dramatically different. In fact, today most foundation officers *expect* their grantees to include a communications strategy in their proposals. Given the value that grantmakers now place on strategic communications, one of the most effective ways to raise money for your work, whether you are requesting funds to help stem global warming or to launch a project aimed at reducing the rate of diabetes in your community, is to include a communications plan and budget in your proposals to funders.

Major individual donors may also be willing to support media outreach efforts. You may be able to develop personal letters or proposals seeking funding for specific aspects of your communications program, such as public service announcements, press kits, and other tangible products. Corporations are another source of income for media projects. If you are working with a company that advertises in the media, it may be willing to negotiate space for your print ads and television time as part of its overall ad buys. Corporations can also be wonderful sources of gifts in kind, paying printing or mailing costs or giving pro bono advice.

Develop Your People Power

Interns and *pro bono* assistance from local public relations and advertising agencies can greatly enhance your program. Here's how to find them:

- **Coordinate internships with local colleges.** Summer interns can be a great help to your efforts. But remember: young people need to be supervised and given instruction so that their learning experiences are productive, skill-building, and fun. A media trend analysis is an ideal project for a college student intern working for school credit. Your best sources of interns will be the journalism and communications departments on local campuses.

- **Check out the university fine arts programs in your area.** If your organization needs a logo and can't afford to hire a designer, or you would benefit from the skills of a Web animator or Web designer, these fine arts programs are promising places to seek interns. You may be able to get the arts program to "adopt" your organization as a project in which students work for credit, or to negotiate some other cost-saving arrangement.

- **Ask retired journalists and media executives for help in developing and implementing your communications plan.** Local advertising and press clubs might help you to identify top professionals with the skills you need. Also try chambers of commerce, senior citizen centers, or local chapters of the American Association of Retired Persons, now known simply as AARP. In fact, the Web sites of local AARP chapters include a feature on the home page that connects organizations to local AARP members who are seeking volunteer work.

- **Request pro bono advertising and public relations support from advertising companies.** Local and national firms traditionally donate time, talent, and resources to nonprofits. The Advertising Council, based in New York City, is a national organization developed to link agencies with nonprofit clients. Your city may have a similar local council or advertising club that can facilitate a partnership. You may want to invite the head or senior partner of a full-service advertising company to serve on your board of directors with the expectation that he or she will provide pro bono services.

You Have Options

There is no getting around the fact that your organization will need to make an investment in communications, but there is no one-size-fits-all communications strategy. What follows is an examination of the resource options for three types of nonprofits. Which most resembles yours?

- Very small, all-volunteer organizations run primarily by boards of directors.
- Small to midsize nonprofits with one to five people working full-time on communications and media.
- Large nonprofits with communications budgets of $10 million or more and with fully staffed communications departments. These include organizations with offices in more than one city and perhaps in more than one country.

Smaller Volunteer Nonprofits

Perhaps you are a small nonprofit with a total budget in the hundreds or thousands of dollars, or a chapter of a national organization, such as the Audubon Society, whose local operations are staffed entirely by volunteers. You can still develop and implement a successful strategic communications plan to enhance your image, raise money, and achieve overall goals.

Let us assume that the board of directors of your group is the driving force. Establish a media committee and ask one of the board members to serve as the chair. Give that person the authority to recruit others to serve on the committee, even if they are not on the board.

A written job description is always helpful in clarifying roles and responsibilities. To be on the committee, a person would need to be able to write, edit, and proofread press releases, brochures, and media kits, and to do graphic design and desktop publishing. By all means include people who are computer savvy. Identify board members who have at least some of the tools of the trade.

If you live in a rural community, there may be few local media contacts, and establishing personal relationships could be relatively easy. You should also reach out to the nearest town or city. If you are in a large city, you will be competing with well-financed organizations who are also looking for coverage. Again, personal relationships will be the key to your success.

Libraries and other public facilities can provide free basic services. Libraries have computers and Internet access. If you need a location for a press briefing or news conference, check out a local community center or library conference room. Or if one of your members works for a law firm, hospital, union, or large corporation, that person may be willing to help find space for events and could possibly even volunteer offices and phones.

Voice mail or an answering machine, and access to e-mail are musts for your media committee chair. These will enable reporters and others to reach you, provided that you can respond to the messages on a regular basis. If your group cannot afford to buy a computer with Internet access, check with law firms, public relations and advertising firms, and major corporations. They may have a computer donation program for their slightly used equipment.

Keep in mind that many grassroots movements in the United States have grown from a small volunteer army to significant agents of change. Eleanor Smeal, president of the Feminist Majority, recalls, "There are times when I think back to when the women's movement began on our kitchen tables. We accomplished a huge amount for women and girls." Smeal now runs a multimillion-dollar nonprofit with operations on both coasts. "As the world grows more complicated, so do our issues. We grew to a global movement for women and additional resources are needed to make significant change today," Smeal added.

Small to Midsize Nonprofits

You are probably on a limited budget. In addition to working with the media, you may have several other duties, such as writing speeches, producing a newsletter and annual report, and overseeing management information systems. You have very little time for actual planning, and you spend most of the day responding to one request after another, most of them internal. Your organization's annual budget is between $750,000 and $2 million, of which 5 to 10 percent is spent on communications. Your goals should be to increase overall spending for communications and to develop a plan that includes approaching funders for a special communications grant. You will also need to convince people that you should be working exclusively with the media and not dividing your attention among six or seven major activities.

Or you might be the national office of a major nonprofit organization with a budget of $3 million to $10 million. Perhaps you are a Planned Parenthood affiliate in a major city, a local United Way, or a statewide cancer organization. You know that your organization has not reached its full capacity and is only responsive to media in 90 percent of its activities. Your board of directors wants more visibility but is reluctant to allocate more funds to communications activities. Your organization spends more than $500,000 on communications per year, so your job might be to develop a plan that makes better use of outside consultants, cuts waste and unnecessary activities, and shows concrete results.

In either of the aforementioned scenarios, the person in charge of media and communications—a press secretary or communications director—should report directly to the executive director, not to someone three or four levels lower down. The senior press staff should have direct access to other decision makers in the organization and would preferably be part of the top management team. If the structure is a communications department with publications, dissemination, and marketing under its charge, then a special press secretary should be part of the team. His or her job should be to work with reporters and implement large parts of the earned and paid media strategies.

Don't assume you need vast resources to be effective in the media, especially if your goals include social change. This bit of wisdom, attributed to Margaret Mead, expresses it well: "Never doubt that a small group of thoughtful, committed citizens can change the world; indeed, it is the only thing that ever has."

Large Nonprofits
Many national and international nonprofits are making serious commitments to their communications activities as a part of their long-range strategic planning processes for the twenty-first century. The United Nations and its agencies, CARE, the National Geographic Society, the

United Way, the Sierra Club, and the American Civil Liberties Union (ACLU) are examples of such organizations. Each has significant staff handling communications, paid media, publications, and regular television and radio productions. For example, the ACLU built a television studio in 2006 and more than doubled the size of its communications department between 2002 and 2005. The Sierra Club has a fully equipped media department to produce documentaries and other audio and visual projects.

Your communications tools might include regular polls and focus groups on select issues, a publishing division, regular television documentaries, news feeds, an art department, a video and audio production studio, media relations, and paid advertising. Communications budgets for large organizations like yours may be in the tens of millions of dollars per year.

Manage Your Team Wisely

The heart of your operation, whatever its size, is the human capital embodied in the people who will actually do the planning, secure the funds, provide the support services, answer the phones, and carry your messages to the media, policymakers, and general public. From the college intern who sometimes answers the phone to the executive director tied up in meetings, they are the face of your organization. Make the most of them through conscientious team management.

Staff and budget management under a communications plan are similar to the oversight conducted for other nonprofit operations. Many books, manuals, and training courses on nonprofit management techniques can be applied to the day-to-day challenges of recruiting and training the right people, monitoring cost controls, integrating computer systems and databases, conducting personnel evaluations, and performing other administrative tasks.

Team management can be especially effective for communications activities. Denise Cavanaugh of Cavanaugh, Hagan, Pierson & Mintz, in Washington DC, has worked as an organization consultant to advocacy groups, service providers, and professional societies. As Cavanaugh tells her clients, "When running a press operation, managers may want to develop a team of people with interchangeable skills. During a press conference, you need all hands on deck—from the top managers to your receptionist. Day-to-day activities like clipping and pasting newspaper articles, however, can clearly be delegated to an entry-level intern."

Each major activity should be included in an overall project work plan that designates the task, the person to whom it has been assigned, the priority it has been accorded, and the deadline. Major projects should have a lead manager to ensure that the work is completed on time, to be accountable for its quality, and to ensure that activities remain within the budget.

Celebrate Success

An important part of building a team is celebrating your successes. If a particularly good newspaper or magazine story comes about as a result of a staff member's placement efforts, have it enlarged and framed for your walls as a tribute to that team member.

Build in time following major projects for feedback sessions so that any problems or mistakes can be discussed and corrected after heat-of-the-moment tensions have passed. Management consultants call this the "philosophy of continuous improvement," based on the concept of "creative dissatisfaction." In other words, even when you have just completed a very successful project or media event, there is always room for improvement. Try to solve your problems without placing blame on people. You will find it more productive to fix the systems or process that posed barriers to success.

Chapter 7

Earning Good Media Coverage

- Cultivate personal media contacts.
- Understand media cultures.
- Pitch story ideas regularly.
- Prepare for media interviews.
- Organize press conferences and briefings.
- Influence the influentials.

Cultivating Relationships with Reporters

Never underestimate the importance of maintaining good media contacts. There is no substitute. The success of any media strategy will depend largely on personal contacts with reporters, assignment editors, public affairs directors, and other members of the news media.

But keep in mind that news media in the twenty-first century have changed dramatically. Journalists who were once considered print reporters working for a daily newspaper are now "news gatherers" filing stories for print, Web sites, radio or podcasts, and possibly video and webcasts. And the nature of the business side has changed so dramatically that the *Washington Post* now describes its profile as "an education and media company, and education is our fastest growing major business."

As described throughout this book, the media industry is constantly changing, and for you to have a successful media strategy, you must understand the culture of your target outlets and maintain strong personal relationships with reporters.

On any given day, you should be prepared to contact a reporter you already know and "pitch" a story or idea to that person. That kind of rapport does not materialize overnight. A steady and reliable relationship can only be developed through regular personal contact and phone conversations. Often this takes months, even years, to evolve. If you are starting from scratch or have just moved to a new city or job, here are some tips for building contacts:

- Establish relationships through other reporters you may know. If you already know someone at a media outlet, ask him or her to introduce you to another reporter, or ask if you can use that person's name when making a cold call.

- Ask all staff and board members if they know any reporters, including relatives, neighbors, high school friends, college roommates, church members, or friends of friends.

- Join local public relations associations so that you can meet reporters through your relationships with other communications practitioners. Many press clubs offer associate memberships to public relations or nonprofit communications professionals. Attend meetings, volunteer on committees, and begin networking.

- Invite reporters to serve on panels at meetings, workshops, and conferences. Because of conflict-of-interest rules, most may not be able to write stories about the event if they are participants, but this is a good way to start a relationship.

- Pick up the phone and schedule a breakfast or lunch if a reporter has done a particularly good piece on your issues. Reporters are usually also looking for new contacts, especially in smaller media markets.

Karen DeWitt has the dual perspective of someone who was a journalist for many years and who has also worked as a senior communications professional for nonprofit organizations. Before becoming the vice president of communications for a large social justice organization in Washington DC, DeWitt covered national politics for the *New York Times* and foreign relations and the White House for *USA Today*, and was a producer for ABC News' *Nightline*. She compares cultivating relationships with journalists to dating, whether it is in the traditional media or in the blogosphere. "You have got to get to know reporters, and the best way to form relationships is to bring something of value to the relationship." That something of value may be a suggestion of a new angle for a story, or contact with individuals with personal stories that will draw in the reader. Like most seasoned communications professionals, DeWitt urges nonprofit communicators to become familiar with the reporters' stories so that you will know what interests them, and to avoid cluttering their mailboxes with information that does not. Take the time to strike up relationships with new reporters and connect them to key players in your organization. "When new reporters attend a press event, it looks pretty much like an insiders' club. They don't know the speakers or the other reporters or the 'players' involved in the event," Dewitt says.

And don't dismiss a reporter because he or she is just out of journalism school. "Novice reporters are often easier to contact and are eager to build a network of sources. Over time, they will rise in the ranks of journalism and become editors and top decision makers," DeWitt adds. Just bear in mind that occasionally, the line between reporter and friend can blur a bit and cause conflict-of-interest situations. Work to keep your relationships professional, honest, trustworthy, and sincere, and you will be able to keep these contacts for life.

Make it easy for reporters to reach you. Get in the habit of putting your home phone number, e-mail address, and cell phone number on business cards and press releases. Many news organizations' deadlines are much later than your office hours, and if there are breaking stories, reporters should know whom they can dependably reach in the evenings and on weekends. Always leave a phone number on your office phone answering system to let reporters know where someone can be reached after business hours.

Maintaining Good Press Lists

Up-to-date press lists are vital. Start by purchasing any and all local media directories. Review newspaper and blogger bylines and magazine mastheads. Watch for credits at the end of television and cable news shows. Keep a journal of all reporters who interview your spokespeople, including business cards with e-mails or cell phone numbers.

Many nonprofit communicators find themselves stymied when faced with the task of compiling a list of bloggers who write about issues that are relevant to their organization. Free Range Studios, a Washington DC–based design firm, whose motto is "Creativity with a Conscience," offers solid tips in the resource section of its Web site (http://freerangestudios.com). We list the highlights here:

- Use both traditional search engines (google.com) and blog search engines (technorati.com) to research blogs.
- Try a variety of issue-related keywords in your search.

- Take advantage of blog directories (for example, www.blogcatalog. com), where dozens of blogs are listed.
- Use blogrolls to your advantage. Many blogs have a feature along the right or left side called a blogroll. This is a list of other blogs that the blogger posts because he or she admires or connects to them in some way. This is an excellent way to discover new blogs that may be relevant to your cause.

A comprehensive press list, organized in a computer database, is a critical tool for maintaining contact with journalists. You can use it not only to update the reporter's contact information but also to store additional information, such as reactions to stories the reporter has written, records of events your organization sponsored that the reporter attended, or notes on who in your organization has good relationships with select reporters. Use your organization's contacts or database software to build your press list. You can also purchase a subscription to a media database from a commercial enterprise such as Vocus.

Low-tech tools can also be used to build press lists. A postage-paid business reply card (BRC) can be an effective way to identify the names of reporters who have an interest in your organization. Include a BRC when sending out your next press advisory on a particularly newsworthy event, a new initiative, the release of a report, or other activities.

Ask reporters to fill out the BRC and mail it back, indicating if they want to receive printed or electronic press materials or to be deleted from your press list. Include a section for additional comments, and you will find that reporters will be very specific about what they want. Any returns will be the beginnings of a "golden press list." Think about it: if a reporter takes the time to do this, he or she has already indicated a very high level of interest in your group or issue.

Snail Mail

Sometimes an old-fashioned letter can work wonders, especially with overseas media, who may not get many letters from the United States.

Andrew Hudson, a fellow with the New York–based group Human Rights First, wanted to establish relationships with U.S. correspondents and others located in Colombia and Guatemala. He wrote them letters (in Spanish where appropriate) establishing the group's aims and resources. He soon found himself being queried regularly by wire services and other reporters who were responsive to the personal touch that his letters gave to his outreach.

To track behind-the-scenes decision makers for specific television news or public affairs shows, record the program's credits and add the names of relevant producers and assignment editors as contacts for your lists. Generally on Fridays, news shows run a full listing of credits. Remember, weekend producers, writers, and assignment desk staffs are often different from weekday decision makers.

When in doubt, call the media outlet directly for correct spellings and for suggestions of whom to put on your press list. Start with public affairs departments, newsrooms, and city desks. If those people are too busy to help you, talk to receptionists.

E-Mail Etiquette

In their slim but highly useful book *Send: The Essential Guide to Email for Office and Home* (Borzoi Books, 2007), authors David Shipley and Will Schwalbe urge a variation of the Golden Rule for e-mail: never send an e-mail that you would not care to receive yourself.

And don't assume everyone gets e-mail on a big desktop computer. "More people than ever before are checking their e-mail on handhelds, which can chop off the ends of subject lines. That's why shorter is better and the first words are key to telling your recipient what you're after" (p. 83).

The authors recommend not using attachments, which take up valuable memory and can carry viruses, when e-mailing reporters.

Reaching Reporters

You should track how best to reach individual reporters and how best to pitch them story ideas. Some journalists, such as Rachel Jones, formerly with National Public Radio, advise nonprofit groups not to send them anything by snail mail unless they have requested it. In a 2007 communications workshop sponsored by the Carnegie Corporation, Jones explained, "Reports and other paper just pile up, and I don't have time to go through it." She prefers phone calls, but only from individuals who have taken time to familiarize themselves with her beat. "Long voice mails are a no-no," says Jones. "I just get irritated and cut them off."

Other reporters, such as Jason Riley, an editorial writer for the *Wall Street Journal,* rarely answer their phones. Riley is always on the run and infrequently works from the *Journal*'s office. His best friend is a handheld BlackBerry, so he prefers to receive e-mails.

There are a variety of ways to make information available to reporters. Every nonprofit organization should have a Web site with a press room section. Surveys are showing that an organizational Web site is a top source of information for journalists, so make certain yours contains pertinent information that is updated regularly and easy to find quickly.

Elizabeth Souder, who covers the energy industry for the *Dallas Morning News,* does not have time to surf the Net, so she relies on a handful of sites that consistently provide information she can use. Best practices for such sites include prominently positioning a "press room" button, or otherwise highlighting a direct link, on your home page for visiting press. At a minimum, the virtual newsroom to which it takes them should include the following:

- *Contact information.* List the name and the contact information for each individual in the organization who has responsibility for dealing with the media. Include the individual's title, area of responsibility, e-mail address, and phone numbers. It is essential to include phone numbers where the press contact can be reached after office hours.

- *Press releases.* Post them in reverse chronological order.

- *Fact sheets.* Reporters do not require a lot of bells and whistles. Provide printable versions that reporters will be able to download as quickly and simply as possible. Text is more desirable than HTML formats because reporters may cut and paste information and quotes.

- *Photos, charts, graphs, and audio or video clips.* Nearly all media today publish and broadcast in multiple platforms. They need photos, charts, graphs, "B-roll" (supplemental video footage to illustrate what is being said in the audio portion of a video story), and audio sound bites—all of which can be posted on your Web site for free use by media. We suggest letting reporters know the options available, and creating a special page in your Web-based press room for easy access to audio, video, and other visual materials.

It is a good idea to alert reporters when new information has been added to your Web site. This is especially true when your organization posts a statement about a news story in which it is involved or that it has the credibility to comment on. Do not wait for the reporters covering the story to find your organization's statement; give them a call or send an e-mail to let them know that it has been posted. Use a teaser quote and include a direct link to your Web site in the body of the e-mail or fax.

Do not bombard a reporter with paper, e-mail, or phone messages, and do not send attachments with e-mails. Attachments are likely to get caught by spam filters, and if the reporter uses a handheld device, he or she may be unable to open the attachment. It's better to send text only, with the link embedded in the text. Keep e-mails short and sweet unless the reporter has asked for more information. Remember, the purpose of the e-mail is to be certain that the reporter is "in the loop" and knows where to find you if he or she wants more information.

You can also forward the reporter published articles from other media to generate additional coverage. Reporters are not averse to borrowing ideas from other outlets. Television news producers often comb the daily papers for story ideas, and print reporters regularly watch television news shows. Veteran journalist and nonprofit communicator Karen DeWitt said one of the first things she learned when she began working at the *New York Times* is how much her fellow journalists trolled local newspapers. "A lot of the *New York Times* news stories percolated from down under." Today, stories also percolate from blogs and social networking sites such as Facebook or MySpace.

Despite the explosion in communications technology, the telephone remains one of your most direct routes for communicating with journalists. Take precautions to ensure that your calls to journalists and their calls to you enhance, rather than jeopardize, your relationships. It is important to be organized. Before you initiate or take any press call, have at your fingertips the appropriate background materials, the names of your spokespeople and other contacts, and the numbers where they can be reached at that moment.

Making the Basic Pitch Call

Most of the time you spend on the phone with reporters should be for calls you have initiated to pitch a story idea, an interview, or an event. Many communications professionals consider this to be one of the most difficult, and least rewarding, aspects of the job. Reporters who don't know you are sometimes abrupt or downright rude, especially when they are in a time crunch. A few of the most successful nonprofit communicators agree that the key to success in pitching a story to reporters you may not know well boils down to one word: "research."

Eric Ferrero has worked as a communications professional for numerous nonprofits, some very large, such as the ACLU, and others that are smaller and more regional, such as Parents, Families and Friends of Lesbians and Gays (P-FLAG). Before contacting a reporter, Ferrero researches the articles he or she has written so as to familiarize himself with the topics and types of stories that are likely to interest that person. "With the state of technology today, it is fairly easy to retrieve a reporter's recent articles and know his or her work before you make the pitch call," Ferrero explained.

"I can still get thrown off if a reporter is hostile, but that's just the nature of the game. The key is not to take it personally. I could have reached the reporter at a bad time of the day," Ferrero added. Abruptness or curt responses do not rattle Ferrero, but pitching a story to a reporter who doesn't cover the topic in question does. "That embarrasses me; it means that I screwed up the research."

There are many online vehicles for researching a reporter's work. One service that is highly effective and free is Google Alerts, a service that delivers news articles directly to your mail box or news reader based on keyword searches. Here are a few additional tips to make pitch calls as successful as possible:

- Assume that the reporter is already on information overload and has probably not seen, or had time to focus on, your press release or press advisory. A personal follow-up by phone is essential. A quick call, even a message left on voice mail, alerts reporters to a specific event and reminds them that your organization is out there and active. If you leave a message, be sure to let the reporter know where he or she can find the press materials on your Web site.

- Reporters will rarely have your press materials close at hand when you call. Be prepared to e-mail them or let the reporter know where to find the information on your Web site. A few reporters may ask you to fax the information, so you should have a one- or two-page document ready to fax upon request. Calls in mid-afternoon or late afternoon are less likely to be answered or returned because of deadline pressure. Morning calls (nine to noon) and early evening calls (after six-thirty) allow more leisurely conversations.

- The rhythm of each news medium is different. The news director at a medium-size radio station starts his or her daily planning long before the sun comes up. A local television station will typically make assignments for that evening's coverage around nine or ten in the morning and start rushing toward a deadline as the five or six o'clock news approaches. If a newspaper reporter is filing for tomorrow's paper, the reporter will typically not welcome pitch calls after four in the afternoon unless he or she needs your quote for tomorrow's story.

- Determine at the outset whether the reporter can talk at that moment. During the morning, you might say, "Do you have a couple of minutes?" In the afternoon, always ask, "Are you on deadline?" If so, ask for a good time to call back.

- Assume that you have sixty to ninety seconds to pitch your event to the reporter. Get to the "who, what, when, where, and why" immediately. If the reporter indicates that more time is available, you can add more information as the conversation unfolds.

- Double-check the reporter's e-mail address or fax number, and be prepared to resubmit your information to serve as a backup or reminder.

- If you have a personal relationship with a reporter, call and offer your spokesperson's reactions to a major event in the spokesperson's field of expertise. Call the wire services and local newspapers routinely with such reactions. They may ask you to e-mail a quote or response to breaking news. Then the reporter or editor will decide whether to use it in follow-up stories. Remember, a wire service like the Associated Press may have many versions of the same story, and your organization might be included not in the first or second story, but in follow-up pieces. This is especially true of major breaking news that might include Supreme Court or state court decisions, legislative action, a crisis, or a natural disaster. These calls may generate interview requests from reporters doing second-day stories.

- If a reporter is especially responsive to your call and seems interested in more information or pursuing your story ideas, suggest that you get together in person over lunch or coffee to discuss the issue more fully, and work with him or her to frame the piece by suggesting other people and groups to interview.

- You should also consider the rhythms of the online version of television, radio, newspapers, and magazines, to which stories are posted throughout the day. If an important news story breaks in the morning, the editor does not have to wait until afternoon deadlines to post it. So don't hesitate to call the reporter if you have information that is pertinent to a fast-breaking event.

Responding to Queries and Possible "Gotcha" Stories

It is a fairly common scenario: a reporter calls late in the day and fires off several questions that you did not anticipate and for which you are not prepared. Chances are that if he or she is near deadline, the reporter already has an idea of the response needed and will keep asking questions until you provide the desired response.

When taking unsolicited calls from reporters, you do have options and can still have an impact on the story, provided your spokesperson is quick witted and disciplined. You should first determine the general drift of the story being prepared and whether the reporter is on a tight deadline. If time is needed to think about options, you might say, "Let me check my files to make sure I have all the correct facts on this, and I'll call you right back" (or establish a mutually convenient time).

After you hang up, write down three points that you want to include in the interview. Call the reporter back at the appointed time, and start by making your points in different ways, but stay on message with your three key points. If the reporter tries to explore other questions, stay on your message to increase your chances of getting the quote you most want in the story.

Do not linger on the phone. Reporters will sometimes extend a conversation, knowing that wary sources will warm up after time. You may be caught saying things you had not planned to say or, worse, things that should not be shared with a reporter. Don't say to a reporter, "I probably shouldn't be telling you this . . ."—just do not say it. Set a time limit and then say, "If we've covered what you needed, I am sure you are busy, and I need to move on to another task. Thanks for calling." Nonprofit leaders often complain that they are misquoted or quoted out of context. More likely, they did say the words and the reporter heard the words, but possibly out of context and with a different intent. Reporters are at liberty to use whichever quotes they choose.

Interview Query

With the rise of highly partisan and sensational cable news talk shows, it is not uncommon for communications staffs at larger organizations in big cities to get very specific queries—casting calls, almost—from bookers and producers looking for a guest who can be counted on to make a particular point. The following e-mail from a national cable network is an example of such a request:

> For Tuesday, we are looking for a guest who wants to "DEPORT ALL THE 12 MILLION ILLEGALS."
>
> Someone who says something like, "TAKE THEM IN NETS . . . OR SEND ARMED GUARDS TO THEIR HOMES . . ."
>
> Someone along those lines.
>
> If you know of anyone, it would be a live television interview . . . between 4–5 P.M. EST.
>
> Thank you.

Taking Phone Messages from the Media

When taking messages from the news media, your support staff, receptionist, interns, or volunteers should find out the name of the reporter, the news organization, and the reporter's deadline. Determine the purpose of the call, the reporter's attitude or tone (if apparent), and his or her phone and e-mail information. The person taking the information should repeat the phone number to the reporter to avoid any mistakes. Not all of this will get asked every time, but setting standards for press calls will emphasize to your entire office how seriously they should take press relations. You might create a standard call form, which can also be used to track names and addresses for your press lists. With reliable records of calls and proper background information on media that are interested in your organization, you can avert a great deal of miscommunication and develop media relations that benefit both you and the reporters.

If your office staff is not properly attuned to incoming news calls, significant opportunities can be missed. This example best tells the story: ABC News' *Nightline* was doing a show on family issues and decided that the head of a New York–based foundation was perfectly positioned to speak about the policy implications. However, phone messages to him were garbled and delayed. When the producers finally reached him, they had already decided to invite him on as a guest that evening! But due to further message mix-ups and wrong phone numbers at his end, the *Nightline* car that was to bring him to the show never arrived (the driver got lost as a result of wrong directions and a wrong address from the organization). The nonprofit spokesperson did not have the name or number of the producer who could have straightened it out. Because of bad staff work, this executive watched in frustration as *Nightline* unfolded before a highly sought audience of influentials, with no mention of his organization and with the wrong slant on the issue. Further, *Nightline* was left with an unfavorable view of the foundation.

Make sure that everyone from the executive director to the entry-level intern in your organization understands clearly that any contact with the media must be handled promptly and professionally. Ideally, just the press office or designated press staff would talk to the media and be in charge of interviews. Incoming and outgoing media calls can either enhance your relationships and your credibility with the press—or ruin them.

Dos and Don'ts for Successful Interviews

Be sure that your spokespeople experience as few surprises as possible when being interviewed by reporters. Pre-interview planning and briefings are important for all parties in the interview before they actually meet with journalists.

Print and Online Interviews

When planning for an interview with a newspaper, magazine, or online reporter, keep the audience in mind. Influentials are more likely to read the editorial and news pages. More women read the lifestyle sections, and more men tune in to finance and sports. Here are a few tips.

Doing Pre-Interview Briefings

The more insights you can give your spokesperson in advance about the reporter, the media outlet, the number and types of stories likely to appear, and the likely questions, the better. Do your homework: locate and review past stories from that outlet on the issues you plan to discuss, especially those covered by this reporter. You might want to rehearse answers to worst-case questions beforehand. Review your message points, as appropriate.

Reporters should also be briefed in advance by a communications staff member so that they do not take up your principal's time with basic informational questions. Brief the reporter on your organization's goals. Send background material, fact sheets, and biographical information. Tell the reporter, "Let me give you all this information as background. I would prefer not to be quoted. Have the official comment be attributed to my boss."

Develop a one-page sheet for the interview that includes the correct spellings of the names and titles of those being interviewed. Also include the correct name of your organization with a three- to four-word description. If you do not do so, a reporter under deadline pressure may get the name or title wrong.

Ask the reporter basic questions: For which outlet will the reporter be writing? A daily or weekly newspaper? The online version? Both? Is there a chance that a wire service will pick up the story in other cities? Will your spokesperson be interviewed by phone or in person? (If in person, select a location most convenient for you, such as in the interview subject's office, restaurant, or hotel.) Will photos be taken? If not, can a photo be supplied by your group? Are others being interviewed for the article? If so, who? How much time does the reporter want for the interview? (The duration of the interview may be up to you, but it should be specified in advance.)

Written background materials should be e-mailed, posted in the newsroom section of your Web site, hand delivered, or faxed, depending on the reporter's preference. The information should be transmitted as early as possible before the interview. Make a last-minute phone call to confirm that it has been received.

Taking Special Precautions for Face-to-Face Interviews

- Have press staff (or volunteers) accompany the spokesperson and sit in on the interview to assist as needed.

- Ask permission to audiotape the interview, especially if the reporter seems hostile. However, never tape without the reporter's knowledge.

- If photos are being taken, remember that the background is a part of the shot. Watch for stray items that may be sticking out behind head shots.

- To avoid misunderstandings, specify any conditions before the interview starts. Spell out what you mean by "background," "off the record," or "not for attribution," as interpretations vary. Avoid going "off the record."

Television and Video Interviews

Television and cable interviews need special attention and preparation to take full advantage of the medium. With television producers and on-air personalities, do not take anything for granted. You will be operating in a very fast-paced environment and must take the time to focus on key details.

Do Your Homework

Prepare your spokesperson for a television interview by watching and taping several past shows. Insist that your spokesperson watch at least one. Check camera angles and the color of the background set. If this is to be a call-in show, alert members of your organization and ask them to participate by making a friendly call or two. If the interview is posted on a Web site with viewer interaction or chat rooms, suggest they e-mail comments and responses. Nearly all television stations and cable shows have viewer comment sections that are monitored by producers, and the results are sent back to decision makers. This can be a good way to generate follow-up stories and interviews.

Stay in close contact with the producer. Be sure that the host or interviewer has a one-page biography of your spokesperson and a fact sheet on your group or issue. This information should be sent to the producer and posted in your Web site's online newsroom. Call the day before to make sure that the producer has the information he or she needs. Make arrangements to tape the interview so that afterwards you can debrief and give feedback to your spokesperson.

Try to meet personally with the host or producer just before the interview in the green room or on the set in case there are last-minute questions. Some producers may ask if there are questions you would suggest that they ask. In some cases, your spokesperson might even be asked just to "talk" into a camera.

Be Flexible

Kathryn Tucker, an attorney for the organization Compassion and Choices, was in Washington DC for oral arguments before the Supreme Court. One major television network news producer told her, "This is a complicated issue and I'm not here to ask any trick questions. Just talk into the camera with the main points you want to get across to the American public, and we will use a sound bite."

This happens frequently. In Kansas City, as a breakfast seminar on family issues was ending, the keynote speaker was approached by a late-arriving local camera operator asking, "My producer just called to say the reporter is caught in traffic. Can you just talk into the camera for a few minutes, and we'll use a piece of it for our noon news?"

With cutbacks in the number of staff in television news rooms, these scenarios are playing out more and more across the country, underlining the need for on-camera training. (See Chapter Nine, "Selecting and Training Spokespeople.")

To make sure you do not make the same mistakes as in the *Nightline* incident related earlier and so that your spokesperson can be informed and prepared, put the following in writing and share it with any staff who might be called into service to support the interview:

- The name, e-mail address, and phone numbers of the station contact
- The name of the host or reporter doing the interview, along with any background information available through a search on the Internet or the outlet's Web site
- The station's call letters, channel, and network affiliation
- The correct address and location of the interview
- The time of expected arrival
- The time the segment will be taped or aired
- The names and background of other guests
- Transportation arrangements and back-up if a car or cab does not show

Mind the Details

Little things count, so check the set, the lighting, and your spokesperson's attire for possible distractions:

- Be friendly with the host, producer, and especially the camera technicians. Their camera angles can make or break the interview. Ask those operating the cameras if they have any last-minute advice to make their job easier and to make your spokesperson look better.
- Find out if it is better to look directly into the camera or at the host. The usual rule is to look at the person speaking. Looking into the camera is often better for remote interviews, where the spokesperson and the reporter are in different places.

- For women, small jewelry, off-the-face hairstyling, and bright clothing in solid colors are best for on-air appearances so as not to distract viewers from the message. Leave dangling earrings and big necklaces at home.

- Make sure the microphone rests in a comfortable place.

- If the interview takes place in a private office or home, the location you choose should be quiet and should have no external noises. Make sure the background is appealing to a viewer's eye, and turn off phones, fans, and overhead paging systems.

- Follow up with a note of appreciation to the producer and the host if it is an especially good segment, and have others in your organization do the same as viewers.

- Don't forget to add the host and producer to your press list.

Briefing the Media

Sometimes you know an event is coming but do not know exactly when. For example, the state legislature is considering an important bill, but a vote has not been scheduled. Or you are planning a gala fundraiser with a number of top celebrities, and you want to alert the media to its importance well in advance. A good way to familiarize reporters with your organization's spokespeople and agenda in anticipation of coming events is to hold a media briefing.

Briefing sessions have a number of advantages over standard press conferences as vehicles for communicating information to reporters:

- You are fully in control of the invitation list and the agenda.

- Reporters can prepare a good story because they have more lead time and more access to your spokesperson.

- A regular program of briefings on important topics can be a powerful way to put your organization's work in the press.

Start by picking a topic. Call four to six reporters and explain that because this issue is on the horizon, you are organizing a "briefing session" for an in-depth look at the issue. Invite two or three experts to speak, possibly some from outside your organization. Ask reporters for a firm yes or no, and be gracious whether they accept or not. You may want to schedule the briefing over breakfast or lunch to keep it informal and conversational. Limit your session to no more than one hour, and allow plenty of time for reporters to ask questions. Provide the basic informational materials, fact sheets, and other written materials. Alert reporters to any new activities by e-mail.

If a reporter says, "I'd love to attend, but I have something else that day," find out when he or she can come, and schedule a second session or a one-on-one meeting.

The Audio Press Conference—a Popular and Practical Alternative

If you are working to reach reporters in different cities, try organizing an audio press conference. It is similar to a regular press conference, but held over the telephone. These normally take at least five to seven days to plan and to make pitch calls to reporters. Planning and promoting the audio briefing will be essential. There are many telecommunications companies with experience in setting up and coordinating audio press briefings.

If you are new to this approach, it helps to know the technical aspects of the audio call and the range of services the company can provide to help you meet your media objectives. To start, the communications vendor will set up a toll-free number for speakers and journalists to call, with enough lines to serve the anticipated number of participants. Speakers will be connected to open, two-way phone lines as they would be for a conference call. Reporters will be on a listen-only line until they signal the operator that they would like to ask a question. Using listen-only lines for a majority of the participants will minimize distractions by suppressing the sound on everyone's lines except for the speaker's. This will block out any background noise going on in the newsrooms and prevent a chaotic, time-consuming free-for-all from developing among participants. The vendor will provide a technician or operator who will work with you to set up the call, open the briefing, instruct reporters on how to signal to ask questions, and remain available until the call is over and everyone is disconnected.

Ideally, someone from your group should moderate. This person will welcome everyone on the call, introduce the speakers, and provide basic information, including your Web address and phone number for follow-up questions. In addition, the vendor can provide a "backline" so that a staff member can talk to an operator (not the person on the call) and can let you know which reporters have signaled to ask a question. The backline monitor and second operator can then determine the order of the questions and who gets to ask a question when.

Prior to the audio briefing, you can make arrangements for the call to be recorded and digitized for use on your Web site as a podcast. Thus reporters who are interested in the story but unable to listen can dial a toll-free number or visit your Web site to hear the proceeding afterward at their convenience.

Costs will vary, but be prepared to pay between $2,000 and $3,000 for an hour-long briefing with lines for twenty to thirty reporters. The cost is based on the number of lines you will require and the length of the briefing.

A successful audio press briefing requires the same preparation as a face-to-face briefing or on-site press conference. Keep the following in mind:

- Determine if there are conflicting events by talking to reporters and by checking out the daybooks in the targeted media markets.

- Notify reporters about the briefing. Do so several times. Send out an advisory about a week in advance, if possible. Put the briefing on the daybooks and news wires. And contact the reporters on your list by phone, fax, or e-mail again a couple of days before the briefing.

- Provide all the basics in a one-page advisory: an attention-grabbing description of the topic, the news context for the event, a list of speakers, and their relationship to the story. Also include an e-mail address and a toll-free number that reporters can use to let you know they plan to "attend." As with a live briefing, post on your Web site pertinent background information that reporters can access, and prepare to fax or send it to any reporter who requests it.

- Hold your briefing while the issue is newsworthy. Audio briefings, like other press events, attract reporters when the news is urgent, groundbreaking, or already dominating mainstream news coverage. Choose spokespeople who are central to the story and whom reporters will be eager to question and quote.

- Gather presenters on a conference call ten to fifteen minutes before the audio briefing is scheduled to begin, for final preparation and coordination.

- Discourage speakers from reading a statement. Rather, they should keep remarks more informal, repeating two to three key points several different ways and offering several memorable quotes and a good ten-second sound bite.

- The audio conference should last between thirty and sixty minutes. Allow ample time for reporters to ask questions.

Tips for Audio Briefings

Nancy Bennett, a freelance communications professional, has organized literally hundreds of audio conferences. Here are a few of her tips to presenters:

- It's even more important to prepare your remarks for an audio conference than for a regular press conference because there are no visual clues.

- Don't use jargon. Don't ramble. The careful use of words and phrases, which is of course important in a regular press conference, is twice as important in an audio conference.

- Prepare a brief introduction for the moderator to use when introducing you. Plan to be available by phone for several hours after the call if reporters have questions while they're writing their stories.

- Use a good-quality land line. Refrain from using a speaker or mobile phone in order to keep ambient sound as low as possible. No one other than the speaker should be talking in the room; turn off any phones or pagers that may ring.

- Identify yourself each time you begin speaking, especially if your voice and the other presenters' voices sound similar over the phone. Start each response with "This is [your name]."

- At the end of the call, the moderator should repeat the name of the relevant Web site and a phone number for more information.

When to Do a Live Press Conference—and Why

A press conference's principal advantage is to eliminate the need for repetitious contacts with many different reporters for a single story. Call a press conference only if you have a legitimate, potentially high-profile news story or must respond quickly to fast-breaking events and are unable to tell your story to reporters one at a time because of time constraints or the large number of news organizations making requests. A press conference is also the right format if you think there is a good chance you will get television coverage.

Conference Call versus Stand-Up Event

The Center on Budget and Policy Priorities is a Washington DC–based group that is renowned for producing timely and credible analysis of developments in Congress and state legislatures that affect low- and moderate-income families. In a given year, the group may produce as many as two hundred separate papers ranging from just a page or two to full-blown reports on census poverty data, to give one example. The Center gets regular, ongoing positive news coverage around the United States.

   Yet in most years the Center holds only one traditional press conference. As the group's Michelle Bazie explains, "Ninety-five percent of the time we can release a report and answer journalists' questions with a single hour-long media call."

Appropriate occasions might include an appearance by a national news maker or celebrity; or a response to a disaster, emergency, or major development that has reporters jamming your telephone lines.

Otherwise, do not call a press conference. For far less time and energy, a series of calls to key reporters can often accomplish the same goals. Too often, nonprofits rush into organizing a press conference only to find that their own people outnumber the handful of journalists who show up. This can hurt morale and send bad signals about your organization or issue to the people who do cover the conference.

If you decide that a press conference is truly warranted, consider the following.

Organization and Preparation

- The more complex your event and the less time you have to plan it, the more important it is to alert the press in writing, so that they will reserve the date. This brief, early "media advisory" is no substitute for the detailed press release that will follow or the even fuller materials you will probably want to hand out at the event. It is a kind of "heads up" to get your event on press calendars, and it can take any number of forms. The daybooks of your local wire services should be among the first recipients of the advisory, as other journalists look to them.

- Ideally, a notice listing the "who, what, when, where, and why" of the event should be posted on the home page of your Web site and mailed or faxed to your press list to arrive three to five working days before the event. Earlier notices are likely to be forgotten, and later ones may not make it onto the reporter's calendar.

- Two to three days before the press conference, use e-mail to send reporters a short release identifying the speaker and the topic. This serves both as a reminder and as background material for reporters unable to attend. Send your notice to assignment desks, national or city editors, and individual reporters. It's usually okay to send releases to more than one person per outlet, as the editors will sort out assignments.

- As noted elsewhere, for your e-mail, put the press release copy into the body of the e-mail in a text-only format. Do not send it as an attachment. News outlets are concerned about viruses, and many screen out any e-mails with attachments. Also bear in mind that most reporters use some sort of handheld device, and it may be impossible or take a considerable amount of time to open attachments.

- The day before your event, try to call all potential news outlets that might attend, explaining that you are following up on the earlier advisory about the event. Start with the AP to make sure you're in its daybook listings of upcoming events of interest to news media. In larger cities, UPI and Reuters may have a daybook as well. Deadlines for daybook listings are usually 3 P.M. the day before, and there is often an advance daybook for the week ahead, with a Friday noon deadline for submission.

- Private press release distributors like PR Newswire are additional vehicles for getting word to the media. There is an annual membership fee and a flat rate for the first four hundred words of any release you want transmitted over its proprietary systems to newsrooms.

Physical Arrangements

Planning is an essential element of a successful event. Focus on the details, from location to room setup. Note the following key activities.

Choosing the Location As a communications professional or volunteer, make a habit of watching national and local television news outlets you are hoping will take your story. See what they cover and what locations provide for interesting television and make for powerful stories. Take your cues from other successful groups.

Hold the press conference in a convenient location or at a site that relates to the news content and that provides a good setting for television. For example, a press conference about housing problems might be staged at a housing project, for maximum visual effect. If you are in a state capital, the capitol building might have a press conference staging room. City press clubs often have rooms available for press conferences. A hotel room or a large conference room might also work, but these do not offer visuals for television other than talking heads, and television cameras often will not come unless it is about breaking news.

Think creatively about the venue. Release a report about early education in a Head Start office or nursery school. If you are releasing an environmental study, find an outdoor location related to your subject matter.

Setting Up the Location Make sure you have enough space, sufficient electrical outlets for cameras, a standing podium, and enough chairs. The space should be slightly smaller than necessary for the number of people you hope will attend. Have staff people ready to fill some seats if required to keep the area from looking empty. Place the podium in front of an interesting backdrop in a location or, if you must be in a plain room, have a backdrop made of a light solid color (preferably blue) with the organization's logo printed in a small repeated pattern so that any cameras can pick up the name of your group or the slogan of your communications initiative.

Preparing for Registration Set up a press registration table and have individual sign-in sheets just outside of the press conference location. Reporters often arrive as a group at the last minute; to keep them from having to wait in line to enter, provide individual sign-in sheets with enough room for legible handwriting. Offer to accept a business card in lieu of a sign-in. The registration table should be ready to operate thirty to forty-five minutes before the press conference starts.

Timing the Conference Generally, press conferences should be no more than one hour long and scheduled to start sometime between 10 A.M. and 2 P.M. (at the very latest). Other periods of the day risk poor attendance because of deadlines and workday starting times.

The National Press Club and Freedom Forum's Newseum

Until 1971, the National Press Club was the exclusive venue for the "men in the media." But today it has totally changed, offering memberships to women and public relations professionals. It is a hub of media activities, with regular luncheon speakers' events on C-SPAN and National Public Radio along with numerous social activities.

Bill McCarren is the general manager of the National Press Club in Washington DC, a few blocks from the White House. Nonprofits in the nation's capital are blessed with excellent facilities for news conferences and strong staff support to help with new technologies. As McCarren describes the club, "We are a modern facility designed for highly effective news events that move key messages to media instantly, digitally and globally. From our state-of-the-art broadcast studios, news conference rooms outfitted with the latest AV equipment, or banquet facilities and meeting rooms, the Press Club deploys professional camera crews, technicians, event planning professionals, food service teams and other professional staff to ensure that your event has the edge it needs to succeed in today's demanding environment."

The club has earned a reputation over the past hundred years for cutting-edge facilities with enough flexibility to meet the special requirements of most groups. Your city may have a press club or other site with comparable appeal.

Also in Washington DC, a few blocks from the U.S. Capitol on Pennsylvania Avenue, is the Freedom Forum's Newseum. The First Amendment is carved into the side of the building as a reminder of the principles of free speech. Each day the Newseum posts the front pages of newspapers from around the world in front of the building; inside, it offers visitors an experience that blends five centuries of news history with up-to-the-second technology and hands-on exhibits.

The Newseum features seven levels of galleries, theaters, and visitor services. It offers a unique environment that takes people behind the scenes to experience how and why news is made. This is a must stop if you are in Washington DC.

Press Conference Basics

One person should be in charge of the event itself, with additional staff or volunteers to help make it a success. The following items deserve attention.

Speakers Limit the number of speakers to three or four at most, and think carefully about the order in which they will speak. A moderator should introduce the speakers and coordinate the question-and-answer period. If possible, designate one or two principals as the main speakers, with the rest available on the podium or in the room to take follow-up questions. Invite the experts on particular policy points to answer questions on those matters, but not as speakers.

Have large name tents made several days in advance for each speaker. If you use a head table and mics, the tents can be important for media identification. Make sure your press kit lists the names, titles, and organizational affiliation of your speakers so that the journalists can correctly identify each one.

Statements Speakers' statements should be crisp and limited to two to three minutes each. All the presentations and speeches combined should last fifteen minutes at most. Leave thirty minutes for questions, or reporters will start to leave. Invite all speakers to bring written statements, and distribute these as part of your press materials. Reporters who do not attend will need these texts to write stories, and any points the speakers omit will be covered in the texts. This minimizes the possibility of misquotes and errors, because reporters have to take fewer notes. The moderator can deliver an opening statement on the purpose of the press conference that makes the headline points. Make sure each speaker has developed at least one good sound bite of no more than ten seconds.

Visuals If you must do a press conference in a hotel room or indoor venue, remember that cameras need interesting visuals beyond people standing at a podium. At a very minimum, do a blowup of your logo for the podium. Position it right under the microphone, not below the logo of the hotel. If you have charts or other visuals in a report, a local photo or copy shop can enlarge them to poster size. Be sure any print is large enough to be read from the back of the room. If you are presenting a video clip or ad campaign, provide a digital file or make broadcast-quality copies to distribute to the television crews that attend. Post any visuals on your Web site. Remember, a television news assignment editor is more likely to broadcast your event if it involves a visual story.

Presentations Ask speakers not to read their statements but to summarize the most important points in a conversational manner. Someone reading a prepared statement can often look unengaged and sound bored. The moderator should make it clear to the speakers as well as the audience that each speaker will talk only for the designated time. If anyone runs over time, the moderator should signal a cutoff and move toward the lectern or otherwise hint that the gong has sounded.

If resources are available, you should produce a digital sound recording and post it as a podcast on your Web site so that absentee reporters can listen to the event afterwards. Or, if you are able to secure a video crew, try doing a webcast for your site so that members, staff, and the public can watch and listen to your event.

Gate Crashers What if uninvited individuals who are not with the media show up, perhaps representing a different point of view from your own? Deciding whether to admit them can be a challenge. As a rule, let them come in unless you anticipate real disruption. If you must bar entry, you have every right to do so. Press conferences are for the working press, not for everyone who wants to be heard. You have some special rights when you have "paid for the microphone."

Follow-Up

Expect to stay after the presentations to meet with reporters who may need additional background or have questions. After the event, take action to follow up both with reporters who attended and with those who did not. Focus on the following activities.

Pursuing No-Shows Check the sign-in sheets immediately after your press conference; then contact the no-shows and direct them to press materials on your Web site. Hand-deliver the information if the reporter requests it. Often this type of follow-up can increase coverage of the press event or stimulate an additional story.

The fact is, some reporters attend press conferences only when there is someone speaking whom they cannot reach by phone. With shrinking newsroom staffs and more assignments than time, reporters at both large and small outlets often skip press conferences and contact the spokespeople after it is over to write their stories. So have press conference participants available for interviews after the event, and be certain to post the materials to your Web site in a prominent location and easily accessible format.

Evaluating the Event Make sure to review what worked at each news event and what did not. Schedule a meeting with key staff as soon as possible to review the organizers' efforts, the speakers' handling of questions, and the resulting coverage or lack of it. This feedback session should also identify the most efficient ways to get press coverage in the future.

Acknowledging the Reporter's Work Under most circumstances, do not thank a reporter for a good story. You do not want to appear to suggest that the reporter was biased. But do call to say, "We appreciate your interest in our work." Stay with a more neutral response.

Correcting Inaccuracies If the resulting story does not accurately reflect your organization's perspective, call the reporter directly to discuss it. Pinpoint inaccuracies, and if they are substantial, ask for a correction. Use a negative story as an opportunity to set up a meeting with the reporter and possibly with his or her editors to discuss overall coverage of your organization or issue. Try to resolve the situation with the reporter, rather than jumping over his or her head to speak to the editor.

If you do not get a response, then a call to an editor or an ombudsman is appropriate. Check the outlet's Web site for places where readers or viewers can comment about a story, file a complaint, or request a correction.

Organizing Major Events

Many groups organize major events—fundraisers, rallies, marches, races, or walkathons—to call attention to an issue or initiative. Media coverage for these events is obviously critical to their success. Advance planning skills and experience are needed to ensure that valuable time and resources are not wasted.

- *Think production.* You or an experienced professional will need to "produce" the event, which means assuming responsibilities not unlike those of a theatrical producer. Earth Day events, marathons, Race for the Cure, and walkathons for AIDS or other diseases are examples of events that can raise money, build awareness, increase memberships, and draw media attention. If they are well staged, they will draw large enough crowds to become hits. If you want thousands of people to attend your event, you might consider linking up with an event planning organization or with media and advance planning professionals from national and statewide political campaigns.

- *Pull out all the stops.* Try to use all the media options we have discussed—media briefings, press conferences, and interviews—to attract advance coverage for your event. Advance planning is the name of the game. Special events take time, money, and creative energy to garner the attention that alone makes such an undertaking worthwhile.

- *Expect gate crashers and alternative media, and decide in advance how you will handle them.* An eleventh-hour barrage of demands for press and VIP credentials is something you can count on, so establish criteria ahead of time for admitting bloggers, newsletter editors, and writers for in-house publications. The Public Relations Society of America recommends treating a blogger as a journalist if he or she has a blog to which a minimum of one thousand sites are linked, but many bloggers with small audiences have high credibility on specific topics. Consider welcoming any who specialize in your issues and who can reach your target audience. Check out the number of links through Internet search engines that track blogs, such as http://technocrati.com.

- *Build in time to produce a memorable event.* Make sure you allow enough time to build a professional-quality stage, rent top-level sound systems, and line up speakers, entertainers, and musicians as your agenda and goals demand. Never try to "wing it" with such an event.

Pitching Your Ideas to Electronic Media

Pitching story ideas to television and cable producers and assignment editors takes special skills. Schedules are tight and resources limited, especially when the economy is down and advertising revenues are tight.

Media Gatekeepers: Tips for Getting to and Beyond Them

Media gatekeepers are the assignment editors and news directors at television stations, and the city, national, foreign, sport, style, or business editors at print and Web media. They are paid to gauge the value of an incoming news idea, and their judgment is often decisive.

The key to catching the interest of an assignment editor in the electronic media is a story idea that combines actual news with good visuals. Your prospects are greatly enhanced if you have cultivated relationships with correspondents and beat reporters.

Talk Shows

Television and cable talk shows are ideal for exploring issues and building awareness of organizations. Many local stations have public affairs programming to supplement their news segments. Cable companies have public access channels for longer, more in-depth discussions. These are good places for your less experienced spokespeople to gain confidence doing interviews.

Appearing on a show is an easy, free, and quick way to raise your issue's visibility or communicate your message. But you will not have control of the show, the direction of the conversation, or the selection of other guests. Therefore, you must be extremely careful about assessing your spokesperson's media-readiness. You do not want him or her surprised by a hostile host who "goes negative" on local or national outlets.

Start by becoming a regular viewer of the show you have in mind. Decide why you want your organization featured, and what goals you want to accomplish. Then try to link your request to an emerging issue or a breaking news event. Local public affairs and talk shows are often guided by national news coverage and may be looking for a local angle. For example, if a national network does a series on health care with an emphasis on heart disease, a local affiliate may be interested in developing a show on heart disease featuring a local expert from a community hospital or university.

News-oriented talk shows, ranging from local cable television round-table discussions to network programs, will be more receptive to addressing social, economic, and political problems. For national issues, contact the individual shows at the major networks directly, and provide background material along with your news "hook." For local issues or events, reach out to local television outlets, including cable talk shows. Although audiences are more limited, local television is more accessible and can provide invaluable exposure for your issue.

You should contact the producer, host, and researcher (if it is a major show) of the program you have targeted. Send a pitch letter along with a press release or press kit, and follow up with a telephone call or e-mail. Most national programs book guests weeks in advance, whereas others wait until immediately before a show is scheduled so as to stay relevant to breaking news. Many talk shows build flexibility into their schedules so that major events can preempt their plans. If a high-profile story breaks that is related to your issue, develop your press pitch and call a talk show to let the producer know of the availability of your spokesperson.

Talk shows present an unparalleled opportunity for your spokesperson to familiarize a mass audience with your organization and issue, but careful preparation is essential. If done well, it can increase the visibility, credibility, and support of your issue and organization.

Webcasts: Your Web Site as Television Station—Almost

A webcast uses streaming media technology to offer videos over the Internet, and may be posted live or recorded. Webcasts are used to post everything from benefit concerts that draw hundreds of thousands of viewers worldwide, to smaller events, such as membership conferences and public speaking events. The costs for developing and posting webcasts vary according to the range of services you require. The cost of a basic package will start around $5,000 and includes one single camera in a conference room or similar venue, taping or transfer to digital format, and transmission in leading webcast technologies. A recording is usually available on demand for up to six months, during which time you can link to the video from your Web site. A live webcast has increased costs and may or may not be critical for your purposes. Two live cameras will provide more interesting visuals, such as shots of the audience as well as the speakers, but some companies will charge $2,000 to $3,000 more for a second camera.

Remember that when producing a webcast, you are producing a video or television show. For it to be successful, you need to produce the program, have good camera shots unobstructed by heads or people jumping up and down, and have a way to identify your speakers, either by name tents or through an editing process costing additional time and money. Even with seasoned professionals producing your webcast, a communications staff person needs to supervise the taping and editing to keep key messages from ending up on the cutting room floor.

Video News Releases (VNRs)

Video news releases (VNRs), also called satellite news feeds, are a part of the toolkit for media strategies with significant budgets. However, after a controversy over a VNR produced by the U.S. government in 2004, the number of television stations that accept VNRs has dropped dramatically. Many companies that produced VNRs for corporate clients found it no longer profitable to do so and discontinued the service.

The situation in question involved the U.S. Department of Health and Human Services' release of a VNR that drew intense criticism from the news industry, which claimed that the VNR misled the public because it ended with the sign-off, "In Washington, I'm Karen Ryan reporting." Ryan was not a reporter; she was a public relations professional. This angered many journalists, who accused Ryan of "faking the news." After a heated debate between public relations companies and the news industry, the

Public Relations Society of America offered the following advice to organizations that produce VNRs:

- Identify the VNR and disclose who produced and paid for it.
- Do not claim, or in any way give the impression, that it is an actual news report.
- Identify the source of any footage not provided by the station that airs it.

If you are inclined to venture into this area, here is what you should know about VNRs. They can range in length from three to six minutes, and generally include the following:

- A short "billboard" of written material describing an issue, the initiating group, and the context of the news feed. This text is produced by a video machine called a character generator.
- A short section of "video news bites," which can include interviews with your spokesperson.
- If available, generic or stock video footage called B-roll (for background), which depicts the situation or event and which is generally used with the station's own voice-overs.
- If available, materials showing how the problem relates to your locality.
- A closing billboard that lists the name and phone number of a press contact for further information.

Planning and follow-through are important in developing VNRs. Actual production of the VNR must be well planned so that the news segment will be ready for the satellite "feed" time. Generally, a video camera crew must be hired either through a local cable system or through a video production facility. The written materials, or billboards, must be submitted to a video editing facility before production so that they can be inserted into the press release. Satellite time must be purchased, and facilities must be secured to uplink the video.

To ensure maximum exposure of the finished product, you should send a promotional letter and fax and make a follow-up phone call to television assignment editors several days before the feed. This notice should include the transponder information, time, date, and a description of the feed. If your organization has local chapters in major cities, it may be possible to organize a coordinated statewide or national promotional effort. Ask members to call their stations, urge them to use the VNR, and offer to help with story ideas.

Getting on the Air: Radio

A handful of local radio stations in each media market have regular news segments throughout the day. Some rely on news syndicates to cover community events, whereas others have a small number of reporters to cover the news. Larger stations in major media markets will have fully staffed news operations. You should understand the implications of these staffing differences.

For example, radio actualities, or audio news releases (described in this section), will be welcomed by small and medium-size stations, whereas stations in larger markets often will not take them. Large stations regularly cover press conferences; smaller stations prefer to do live or taped interviews. A small operation that does not take radio news feeds might agree to conduct an interview in its own studio.

Talk Radio

Talk radio is an important programming component for many radio stations. Generally, stations specializing in talk radio try to respond quickly to emerging local or national issues.

When booking a radio talk show, contact the show's producers and researchers, in addition to the host doing the segment. Timing this media event right and knowing how to pitch your story in terms of its local or state-based news angles are critical. Generally, an issue advocate can expect substantial coverage of his or her issues on talk radio if producers and hosts receive proper advance materials. Often it is not necessary for the guest to visit the studio, because a good-quality interview can be done by phone. This format is an especially good one for local groups because it is conversational and does not require proficiency at delivering thirty-second sound bites.

Keep in mind that a majority of radio stations now stream their programs on the Internet in addition to broadcasting over the air, meaning they can now be heard around the world in real time. Many stations also post programs as podcasts, creating radio-on-demand and allowing you to link to them from your organization's Web site.

Radio Tours

One of the greatest advantages of radio is that a spokesperson can be immediately connected to a potentially vast audience with nothing more complicated than a telephone. Sometimes a large radio station or network will want your spokesperson to arrive for an in-studio interview.

But for most local stations, a telephone call is the preferred method. In short, radio is a fast-turnaround, inexpensive, and easy vehicle for reaching demographically discrete audiences. What's more, some spokespeople are far more comfortable in a radio interview setting, where they need not worry about appearances. One union president liked to joke that he preferred early morning radio interviews so he could conduct them "in my pajamas."

A radio tour is a series of interviews conducted by telephone with many stations during a given period of time. Publicists for national celebrities, such as best-selling authors, use them as part of their launch strategy for new books. The author will be brought into a professional recording studio to block out sounds that can interfere with an interview. The studio will have special phone lines and switching equipment that permits rapid connection with as many as forty different stations in a single session over a full day.

The first interviews are scheduled for critical drive-time hours, beginning at 5 A.M. Eastern Standard Time. The interviews follow the rising sun across the nation until they end at 9 A.M. Pacific Standard Time. A national radio tour can reach a huge percentage of the national radio audience in a single morning, and the spokesperson need never leave his or her own city.

This more expensive, technically advanced radio tour can easily be adapted to smaller budgets. Simply limit the interviews to the city, state, or region you wish to reach, and instead of a special studio, use a quiet office and phone line. This can still be a daunting task in populous states with hundreds of stations, however. Another way to reach many stations with a single call is to book an interview with a state radio network. Large state networks can reach as many as a hundred stations with their news feeds.

The traditional pitching of an interview to a radio producer requires a tremendous compression of your story lines. A typical producer may know within thirty seconds whether he or she wants to book your spokesperson. You should be ready with a one-page fax with pithy quotes and a short bio of your spokesperson for immediate follow-up. Be prepared to change and update the calendar on scheduled bookings; radio interview slots are famous for last-minute shifts.

In the summer months, keep a special eye out for talk show opportunities on stations that carry baseball games. If games are rained out, they often substitute talk shows and will be looking for guests to appear on very short notice.

Radio Actualities

Radio news actualities, which are audio press releases, are excellent tools for nonprofits because of their relatively low cost and quick turnaround times. Unlike the challenges associated with video press releases for television as described earlier, radio releases have become a standard news device for smaller and medium-size radio stations. Usually no more than sixty seconds in length, the radio news actuality typically features a short "news bite" on an issue, a quote, and a suggestion on how to obtain more information, usually with a phone number.

At a cost of approximately $3,000 to produce and disseminate and with one or two days' advance work, a single radio news actuality can be distributed to and carried by half the radio stations in your state. Here are the most common elements of a radio actuality:

- A short "wraparound" giving the "who, what, when, where, and why" of the news event

- A sound bite of about thirty seconds featuring your organization's spokesperson

- A "trailer" giving the name, e-mail and Web address, and phone number of the media contact at your organization

Talking Back to Your News Outlet

Local and national broadcast news programs and cable magazine shows regularly have segments that allow feedback from viewers. This may consist of letters or e-mails from viewers or chat rooms on program Web sites. Some chat rooms make it possible for viewers and listeners to interact with journalists and prominent news makers. Feedback segments provide an excellent opportunity for you to deliver messages directly to people who can disseminate them further. Watch, read, listen, and surf the Internet for ways in which your members—professionals, advocates, experts, or consumers—can have an impact on media decision makers.

The Benefits of Radio

Radio can play an important role in your media strategy. It offers a proactive way to reach out to targeted audiences and familiarize them with your organization and issues. Radio is relatively inexpensive and fairly easy to access. It offers more time to expose your organization's point of view than any other medium, and it is particularly effective in suggesting an action that people can take, such as becoming a member of your group, writing to an elected official, or sending in donations. As one element of your overall media strategy, radio offers an opportunity to give your spokespeople, your organization, and your issue valuable exposure.

Showcasing Your Ideas in Newspapers

Newspapers of all sizes and circulations set aside space for readers to share their comments and ideas. Members of your organization should be encouraged to submit letters to the editor and opinion pieces on a regular basis. Here we discuss the nuts and bolts for successful placement.

Op-Eds

For nonprofit groups and government agencies that lack the advertising budgets to buy access to top decision makers, an op-ed placement can be invaluable. It is not, however, without its challenges.

Placing an Op-Ed: What Editors Want

A handful of newspapers have opinion sections capable of influencing the national debate. The *Wall Street Journal* and the *New York Times* all have printing plants in every region and have vast circulation among the most politically engaged and influential Americans. These papers are available in most major cities, but each one approaches outside op-ed contributions in different ways. The *Journal,* for example, tends to feature one or two opinion pieces each day right next to its own editorials and is much less likely to run articles that run counter to its own official positions.

Despite their many differences, these and other papers are deluged with submissions every day, and many look for local or regional approaches to national issues, or something even closer to home. Learning what they want and how to provide it is a first step in entering the marketplace of ideas.

Op-ed editors usually have some very concrete requirements for selection. Timeliness is an important consideration. Even if your op-ed does not break new ground, you may be able to find a news hook: a holiday, an anniversary, an election, an upcoming conference, a report, a vote in Congress, or pending action by local or state government. Editors want opinion pages to be relevant to ongoing events. If properly crafted, your op-ed can help achieve this goal.

The author's byline can make a huge difference. Having the article signed by a local or national expert, your group's president, a member of the clergy, or a well-known politician could enhance its prospects of being printed.

Editors also tend to look for the following:

- A provocative idea on any subject
- An opinion on a current issue that is controversial, unexpected, authoritative, or newsworthy
- A call to arms on a neglected subject
- Bite and wit on a current issue

Op-ed pages do not run announcements of events, status reports, or the blatant promotion of organizations or obscure causes. Most editors seek sharp opinion, advocacy, denunciations, controversy, and surprise.

Investigating Submission Requirements

Nearly all newspapers post on their Web site instructions for submitting an op-ed. Most are very specific about the length (usually between 500 and 650 words) and spell out submission requirements in detail.

For the quickest access to the op-ed specifications for the nation's top one hundred newspapers, go to www.ccmc.org, the Communications Consortium Media Center's Web site.

Writing Your Op-Ed

The first step in writing an op-ed is to think through what message you want to deliver. What is your goal—to recruit volunteers, start a grassroots initiative, sustain or increase public funding, pass new legislation, or educate opinion leaders and the public?

Defining the goal will help you determine which audience you need to reach: the general public, local or national policymakers, or specific groups, such as voters, teachers, health care professionals, or senior citizens. Defining the audience will also help you determine which outlet the op-ed is best suited for: your local daily or weekly paper, a professional journal, a state or regional paper like the *Denver Post* or the *Boston Globe,* or the much more competitive national papers, such as the *New York Times.*

Here are helpful hints to consider when writing the op-ed:

- Try to reduce your point to a single sentence. For example: "Every child deserves a family," or "White Americans receive better health care in the United States than African Americans and Latinos. Why?" See if your sentence passes the "wow" test or the "hmm" test; if not, the point needs sharpening.
- Any point worth making will have to be defended. Muster your best three or four supporting arguments, and state each one in a single paragraph. Be as specific as possible.

- Avoid starting sentences with "There are." Use the active voice rather than the passive voice.

- Raise your opponents' best arguments, and challenge them with countervailing facts, withering irony, condescension, or whatever is appropriate, but address them.

- What is the minimum background information a reader absolutely has to have in order to grasp this point? Write no more than two paragraphs that summarize this information.

- Imagine your target reader browsing the newspaper on a workday morning, hoping to find something interesting. What kind of statement might catch this person's attention? If you can raise questions or surprise, intrigue, or baffle your reader into getting past the first paragraph, you stand a chance that the editor will put your op-ed in the paper.

- Now write the piece. Draft about a thousand words (four double-spaced pages) maximum. Restate your key points in the final paragraph.

- Cut out half a page. Eliminate repetition. Trim words, not ideas. Check every word to see what you can eliminate. Convert passive verbs to active ones. Give the piece to someone else and ask that person to review it. If rewriting or cutting is required, you want to do it yourself, rather than leave it to the discretion of the newspaper editor.

- Your final piece should not exceed 750 words. In fact, many newspapers require the piece to be even shorter.

- Do not forget to include your name, title, and affiliation at the end. Submit the piece with a short cover letter that includes your name and phone number. You will be notified if your article is accepted for publication. Calling and badgering the op-ed staff may not help and could hurt you. Be patient. It can take weeks for even a time-sensitive op-ed to appear. Stay ready to update and revise in the hours before publication.

If your op-ed is rejected, revise it and try another publication. Or try again in a few weeks or months on another topic. Do not despair. Your piece may have arrived during a very busy week with lots of competition. Often it is just a matter of your op-ed's being in the right place at the right time.

If your piece is printed, make copies and send them to colleagues, elected officials, funders, reporters, and others who can help move your issue. This can be an excellent way of getting your exact message to key influentials and of helping frame the debate. An op-ed can serve as a springboard to talk show appearances, panel discussions, and countless other opportunities.

Keep in mind that most U.S. news outlets have some mechanism to let viewers and readers express their opinions on important issues: op-eds, freelance articles, essays, online chat rooms, e-mails to reporters, or letters to the editor. Using these outlets, you have an opportunity to position an issue or frame the debate in your own words. Moreover, for every letter, e-mail, or comment a news outlet receives, it assumes there are hundreds, if not thousands, of readers, viewers, and listeners who feel the same way. Thus even a few strongly felt letters can carry a great deal of weight.

Editorial Boards: Influencing the Influentials

A newspaper's editorial position, whether the paper is a small weekly or major daily, can have an enormous impact on public opinion and public policy because of the ripple effect on readers, decision makers, and important influentials in a community.

A small newspaper's positions on issues are decided by the publisher or managing editor. Editorial positions at larger newspapers are decided by a group of editorial staffers known collectively as the editorial board. Editorial boards consist of some or all of the following people: the publisher, the editor-in-chief, the managing editor, the editorial page editor, and editorial writers. You should ask for an editorial board meeting whenever an issue important to your organization is being debated, and it's not always necessary to meet with the full board to make the case for editorial support. Sometimes you can get a meeting with the board member who writes the editorials on your issue, says Jason Riley, editorial writer for the *Wall Street Journal*. That can work just as well.

Whatever route you take, it is important to know whether the paper has already taken a position on your issue or published previous stories or columns related to it. You can gather this information by searching the newspaper's online archive, a database of news articles such as LexisNexis, or Google.

If you have never coordinated an editorial board meeting, call one of the editorial board writers or the secretary to the editorial page editor. Describe your organization and indicate that you would like to arrange an editorial board meeting to discuss why it is important for newspapers to take an editorial position on this issue. It is very important that you are clear that the purpose of the meeting is to "ask" the paper to take a position and to write an editorial. Unless you are clear about what you want them to do, you may be wasting your time and theirs.

If the paper is large, you should call at least a week to ten days in advance. If it is small and does not have an editorial board, suggest a meeting with the publisher or editor, or propose an informal get-together over coffee or lunch.

At the meeting, present a statement of your organization's position on the issue, one or more fact sheets supporting your position, and the names and numbers of spokespeople who can be contacted for further information. Ideally, you should limit the number of people you bring to the meeting to two or three.

Because many smaller papers limit their editorials to local issues, you should be prepared to stress from a local perspective why a particular policy needs to be adopted and, again, why the newspaper should take a position on the issue. In many ways, meeting with an editorial board or an editor is not much different from meeting with your member of Congress or another elected official.

You may be asked when proposed legislation is likely to be voted on, why it is needed, why your organization is supporting the legislation, and so on. If you are unable to provide detailed information, say that you will get back to them with the information, and check your organization's national office; maybe it can help out.

If the paper runs a favorable editorial on pending policy issues, immediately make copies and send one to your member of Congress at the district office and in Washington DC. Also send a copy to your organization's national office in Washington so it can send a complete package of editorials to other members of Congress. Likewise, if you are working on a local initiative, send copies to mayors, council members, governors, or state legislators.

Columnists

What do George Will, Clarence Page, and Maureen Dowd have in common? They are nationally syndicated columnists who are paid to write their opinions and whose writing is carried in newspapers throughout the country. They are not news reporters; their role is to draw conclusions and not to cover stories in an unbiased manner.

The most widely known columnists are syndicated, which means that their work appears in more than one publication. They sell their columns to a syndication service, which markets them throughout the country. This system enables small newspapers to feature big-name writers while providing columnists with significantly larger audiences.

Nonsyndicated and local columnists usually write for only one paper, but may also write blogs for their online editions and appear on local or national talk shows; thus their power should not be overlooked.

It is critical to be familiar with a columnist's positions before you make contact. When you have identified a columnist who might support or write about your issue, try to develop a relationship that will enhance your mutual interests, and suggest stories that are timely and relevant.

Blogs

As noted elsewhere, there are bloggers who write about politics, the arts, television, or their personal passions. Some are news aggregators. They collect the news that will interest their readers and post it on their blog. A small number are news generators, meaning that they generate their own press stories. Blogs can help nonprofit organizations get out their message. You may find that a blogger will be able to move a story that you had no luck pitching to mainstream media, or that including a blog on your organization's Web site can increase traffic and attract return visitors. Consider recruiting a well-known expert on your organization's issues to write a blog on a regular basis, and include blogs as a part of a comprehensive communications strategy. Send bloggers your press releases and cultivate them as you would newspaper reporters, but realize they are usually free spirits with very specific ideas and points of view. (For additional discussion on blogs, see Chapter Five, "Navigating a Changing Industry.")

Taking the Next Step

The activities and tips outlined in this chapter are tried-and-true methods of getting your message out using earned media. But the best communicators do not solely rely on the tried and true; they are always honing their skills and looking for new approaches that will put their organizations ahead of the pack. A good way to find fresh ideas is to meet regularly with other nonprofit communicators. Arrange lunches and after-work sessions to share ideas. Celebrate your successes, drink a little wine, and whine about the not-so-successful project. In the end, this will not only make you a better communicator but also help strengthen the capacity of the nonprofit community.

Chapter 8

Responding to a Media Crisis and Managing Backlash

- Develop crisis response systems before a crisis happens.
- Plan for worst-case scenarios.
- Learn to manage a media backlash during crisis and controversy.

UNFORTUNATELY, PEOPLE MAKE mistakes, systems break down, and organizations do not always perform according to expectations.

Thus a crisis turned public with extensive media exposure can occur at any time, causing long-term damage to individual reputations and organizations. For public agencies and nonprofits responsible for people's safety and well-being, even a slight error can have devastating consequences. "If it bleeds, it leads," some pundits say of the local news operation, not entirely in jest.

Any of the following scenarios (drawn from actual news headlines) can quickly undo much of the good you've struggled to achieve:

- People die unnecessarily or are seriously injured while in the care of a public agency or nonprofit contractor.
- A nonprofit is sued for violations of civil rights, fair labor standards, or other employment-related charges.
- Sexual exploitation is revealed by your employees or affiliates.

- Interpersonal tensions explode. National boards of directors or local chapters may be caught in an internal battle, with one side using the media as a weapon to build public sympathy.

- Serious mismanagement of funds is disclosed by whistle-blowers or investigators, exposing your organization to public scrutiny and a challenge to its tax status.

- Emergency situations or natural disasters occur. This is often a time when numerous organizations appeal for and dispense large sums— followed at some point by clamors for accountability. If funds go awry or are not helping those in need, a public scandal can erupt. The massive global coverage of FEMA and its inadequate response to Hurricane Katrina, to cite one example, led to congressional hearings, the resignations of agency heads, and special investigative commissions.

It is important to understand not only that crises occur in the best-managed and best-staffed agencies but also that systems can be set up so that quick and quality decisions can be made to soften their impact.

This chapter is designed to help you identify a risk before it turns into a tragedy leading to media frenzy, and to help you deal with a crisis when it occurs. It focuses on four areas of crisis communications management: (1) a crisis communications plan, (2) prevention and risk management, (3) roles and responsibilities, and (4) possible scenarios. It then discusses ways to counter backlash.

Gearing Up for a Crisis

When dealing with the media, one must be organized, professional, and truthful. The thing most likely to damage an organization's image, even in the wake of a scandal, is making false or ill-advised statements to the media.

Be prepared for the unexpected at any time. In a true crisis, a crisis communications plan that anticipates the worst, is well thought out, and is ready to be implemented at a moment's notice can be your most valuable resource.

The biggest mistake you can make is to assume that a crisis brings chaos in its wake. To weather a crisis with minimal damage, you can set systems and procedures in place now that will continue to provide a framework for action, even if the individuals in charge are caught by surprise.

The three basic rules of a crisis communications plan are (1) prepare for the worst, (2) remain calm and in control if a crisis happens, and (3) be proactive after it occurs.

There are several steps you can take as a precaution, before a crisis happens:

- Invite staff and colleagues to participate in the development of a plan. They will be more supportive of a plan they helped create, and won't be paralyzed when a crisis hits.

- Form an internal task force. Some people are better than others at keeping calm and focused on what needs to be done when those around them are distraught. Meet with these people regularly as a group to discuss strategies for dealing with upsets.

- Make sure everyone knows what to do if a crisis occurs: Who makes what decisions? Who responds to media?

If you put efficient systems in place, things won't fall apart when something goes wrong. At those times, it is more important than ever to

- Stay in control.
- Keep your target audience in focus.
- Have clearly developed messages.
- Have clearly defined roles.
- Decide who will speak with the media.
- Monitor media coverage.
- Maintain internal communications.
- Provide a quick analysis of the situation and its impact.
- Be truthful and honest.
- Prepare background documents in advance. These will be similar to those in your press kit, but will address the situation at hand.

Preventing a Crisis by Identifying Risks and Managing the Situation

The key to managing a crisis is prevention. Because every organization faces difficult, volatile, or controversial situations that may turn sour in the media, your crisis communications plan should be carefully thought out, covering all foreseeable situations. The best approach is to identify potential risks and to manage them before they get out of control.

When a crisis occurs, the organization must be prepared to act, not react. The speed, forthrightness, and skill with which managers and designated spokespeople meet these imperatives will have direct bearing on public and employee opinion. Although crises can damage an organization's image, they also present opportunities to represent an organization as honest, professional, and steady under fire.

But keep in mind that tax-exempt status is awarded as a public trust. Nonprofits will be held to a higher standard than corporations in relation to finances, safety, and service to your community. If there is a lack of transparency or even a hint of cover-up, the media will rightfully become the watchdogs for the public. An interesting resource is the Institute for Crisis Management (ICM, http://crisisexperts.com), a company that provides crisis communications planning, training, and consulting services to business clients as well as nonprofits, health care providers, and higher education. ICM releases an annual report based on news coverage of business crises, and, in its June 2007 newsletter, ICM president Larry Smith discussed lessons learned—some of the very best available to any organization:

> *Two-thirds of all crises should never make it to the level of "crisis." From the top of the management chain to the bottom of the organization food chain, everyone should always be on the lookout for those little problems or issues that, ignored, or under-estimated, can grow into a full-blown public nightmare. This rule applies to everyone from General Motors to Genny's Diner and from the University of Virginia to the Westside Battered Women's Shelter. However big or small your company, school, hospital or non-profit, you should have a crisis operations plan, a communications plan and a business recovery plan and in a perfect world, those three plans would be integrated into one document and it should be kept up-to-date and tested regularly.*

Given the importance of planning for a crisis, it is useful to start your planning well in advance with a risk assessment exercise to help you recognize and address potential problems. Divide a sheet of paper into two columns. On the left side, list the operations within your organization that are likely to present problems leading to a crisis. On the right side, suggest preventive measures to address those vulnerabilities.

Managing a crisis entails knowing what to do when a crisis happens, what to do afterward, and how to work with the media throughout. You

---

Scenario Planning

As part of your advance planning, ask your crisis team to identify high-risk scenarios that have been faced or that might be faced in the future. For each real-life scenario, examine or try to determine the following:

Scenario: What would constitute a bona fide crisis in your organization, and how might such a situation unfold?

Assumptions: What assumptions could the press, the public, and the staff expect to hold in this situation?

Crisis team: Who should be on the crisis management team? Who will make the assignments?

When to act: When should the crisis management team be activated?

Strategic objectives: What do you hope to accomplish with your statements and actions?

Strategic message: What message do you most urgently need to convey? To what audiences?

Actions: What concrete actions will you take to contain the crisis and to prevent a recurrence? What evidence, if any, do you have that this will work?

Examples of Scenarios

- A child dies while in the custody of a children's services agency.
- A volunteer or employee is charged with sexually abusing teens in the program.
- An environmental group is charged with polluting the local water supply.
- An animal escapes from its cage at a zoo or local circus and injures or kills a member of the public.
- Your organization is accused of mismanaging $1 million in government contracts.
- Groups opposed to your mission are determined to discredit you in the media by misrepresenting your positions on controversial issues or by misrepresenting your finances as being wrongfully spent, to make your group "radioactive" with donors, supporters, elected officials, and the media.

---

cannot afford to neglect any aspect of a crisis. Here are some general rules to remember:

- Develop a crisis management plan before a crisis happens.
- Define basic operating principles from the beginning; for example, don't lie to the media. Stage a "crisis drill" to be sure that each staff member understands what is expected of him or her.
- Be prepared at all times to field a call from the local media about an emergency, a scandal, or some other negative event. Develop a standard reply in advance that does not put you in the position of saying, "No comment." The reply should be developed collectively with your crisis communications team.
- Develop clear messages that focus on a concern for people who may have been affected or hurt, not programs. Acknowledge that a problem

has occurred, and show compassion for any victims or family members involved. The initial statement should not assign blame but rather should assure the public that you recognize the seriousness of the situation. It should indicate that not all of the facts are known and that a full investigation will begin immediately to prevent the situation from recurring. Meet emotion with emotion.

- Present a spokesperson with good media skills based on media readiness training. If the crisis is extremely serious and involves loss of life or significant mismanagement, your spokesperson should have media training before engaging with any national reporters and especially with any television and video reporters.

- Refer all media requests to a single office or official spokesperson. Develop a written message or "talking points" memo for responding to crisis-related phone calls. If a reporter is doing a story based on false information, set the record straight in each conversation. Don't assume that the reporter has the full picture.

- Monitor local media coverage as the situation unfolds. Make recordings of television news coverage with TIVO or other equipment, and track print coverage, including influential blogs, by going online several times a day. Carefully read the various editions and updates appearing online for both early and late editions of local publications. Local and national bloggers can also have an impact on coverage of any crisis—they may cause backlash to occur.

- Form a proactive media team to correct inaccurate information that appears in the media. Request retractions if necessary. Make sure your Web site is updated regularly with accurate information, and triple-check the information available on your Web site if a crisis unfolds. Do contact names and numbers need to be removed or updated?

- Be available twenty-four hours a day. Position yourself to the public as helping the media obtain accurate information. Under no circumstances should you or the organization appear to be covering up or trying to distort the facts.

- Assume that reporters are in contact with numerous sources of information, starting with in-depth searches on the Web and including police records or visits with neighbors, family members, public officials, eyewitnesses, and even your staff. Reporters often do extensive online and telephone research. If the stories escalate and continue, news outlets will add more reporters to their coverage. Some may not have any knowledge of your organization, your mission, or how it operates. Be prepared to answer the most basic questions repeatedly.

- Immediately identify adversaries who regularly talk to the media and are likely to be critical of the situation, so that you can anticipate what responses may be needed. Call supporters and ask for their help in working with the media. They can be important validators and can help turn around media coverage.

Priority Objectives in a Crisis

Although every crisis has different elements, many cases related to social service agencies have common aspects that lend themselves to specific strategic objectives and supporting messages. Where families are involved, those objectives are often to

- Ensure that the family members of victims or affected individuals are notified immediately, tactfully, and properly, and provide support for the family in dealing with the tragedy

- Ensure that young family members are shielded from intrusive media attention

- Cooperate fully with law enforcement officials to bring an alleged perpetrator to justice or to stop the violation of laws

- Provide appropriate support for innocent staff members and supervisors

- Review the situation for potential liability issues, and implement strategies for addressing them

- Minimize damage to the organization's operations and reputation

- Set the record straight or rebuild public confidence in your organization after being scandalized in the media

Strategic Messages in a Crisis

As noted earlier, one way to think strategically about messages is to imagine how the news media might play the story. This exercise is equally important in the heat and confusion of a crisis situation.

Ask yourself, What do you want the headline in tomorrow's paper to say? What would the worst conceivable headline be? What is the best you can expect, given the situation? Also ask yourself, was this the first such case or the latest in a horrible series? What actions were taken in the last such incident, and are they appropriate now? What public officials or organizations can be approached for assistance in preventing a recurrence?

As difficult as it may be, remember that others will not judge you by the fact that you encountered a crisis but by how well you handled it.

A Short-Term Communications Strategy

A short-term strategy at the beginning of a crisis would be to follow three basic steps: be accountable, take action, and commit to change.

Be Accountable

- Feel the pain. Acknowledge that this is a bad situation. Show the emotions anyone would feel—shock, grief, remorse, condolence. If appropriate, visit family members and make it clear that their well-being comes first.
- Do not appear to be covering up. Accept responsibility; offer an apology, if appropriate.
- Be accountable and do not scapegoat.

Take Action

- Do something. Bemoaning a lack of resources or blaming others is not recommended; it is perceived as whining. Describe a plan. Announce a full investigation. Report back to the media later on its implementation.
- Ask for help from the community, but do not in any way implicate the community in what has happened.
- Be prepared for questions as to why a potentially dangerous situation was not noticed earlier.

Commit to Change

- Accept responsibility, show concern, and explain that changes will be made so that it will be harder for this situation to happen again.
- Implement the changes and monitor their effectiveness.
- Observe how others handle crises, and learn from them. If your organization faces crises often and it is up to you to become a crisis expert, make a point of watching closely how other groups manage during a crisis. When a plane crashes, for example, it is very important that an airline show special consideration to family members. In political scandals, it is critical to avoid charges of a cover-up or obstruction of justice. If people get sick or die from eating contaminated food, focus on the response of company spokespeople. Were they convincing and sincere, or did they appear cold and uncaring? Apply what you learn from such damage control cases to your own organization.

Setting Roles and Responsibilities

The executive director and senior communications staff must work together effectively. They have the primary responsibility for investigating and managing any internal situation that could develop into a crisis, and speak for the organization during a crisis.

- Be prepared to talk about what is happening. You do not treat the press as an enemy under normal circumstances, and that shouldn't change now.

- "No comment" will not get you off the hook. It is far better to admit that you were caught by surprise or even that things look rather grim than to refuse to answer media questions. A "no comment" or nonresponse will only make reporters wonder what you have to hide, and they will report that in their stories.

In a crisis, the executive director should do the following:

- Assemble the crisis team and make or delegate staff assignments and policy decisions related to the situation.

- Ensure that current operations are meeting all standards.

- Shield family members affected by the situation from intrusive media attention.

- Contact and brief board members, local administrators, and other officials as needed.

- Review potential liability issues, obtain legal counsel, and implement appropriate actions.

- Formally request a review of any suspicious death or injury by the appropriate authorities.

- Personally contact the staff, workers, and supervisors involved in the situation to ensure that they have support from the organization for the duration of the crisis, assuming there is no crime or wrongdoing.

In a crisis, the director of communications should do the following:

- Respond to all media inquiries and communicate strategic messages.

- If necessary, ask for media cooperation in withholding identifying details until the next of kin are notified.

- Meet with designated spokespeople to reevaluate the communications strategy as the situation progresses.

- Try to determine what reporters already know, what angles they are pursuing, and, if possible, where they are getting their information.

- Review your Web site for accurate information and as a vehicle for getting your story out in the best possible light.
- Monitor media coverage throughout the days (and weeks) of the crisis.

Crisis versus Controversy

Recognize the difference between a crisis and a controversy. Media regularly cover controversy, and reporters see controversial issues as news. It is important to distinguish working on controversial issues like immigration or abortion from being caught in a serious crisis. When people come to complete agreement on a course of action, it stops being controversial. But most of the activity on social issues takes place in a context of contention. That is natural enough because social issues of concern to nonprofits and public agencies tend to raise fundamental questions about the roles, rights, and responsibilities of governments, families, and individuals.

As a communications strategist, you will encounter setbacks brought about by factors outside your control. A single event or a series of them can negatively change the tone and focus of the media's coverage of your issue. Even in the absence of unfavorable events, critics may attack your messages to get attention and hurt your cause. This is when framing an issue becomes an important skill. Often, whoever frames the debate, wins the debate.

Any number of developments can trigger a backlash. Reporters might attempt to cover an issue from all sides; for example, even though seven in ten people supported an Equal Rights Amendment to the Constitution, it was defeated by a handful of opponents who got equal time for spurious arguments about women in combat and coed bathrooms.

Whatever the cause, a backlash is something that most communications strategies must anticipate.

Once a backlash based on controversies starts, it can be hard to turn around. There is an old saying that journalists are like crows on a wire; when one flies off, the rest will follow. Pundits may feel free to make predictions based on the trend-spotting conventional wisdom of other journalists like themselves. A bad event can quickly spiral into a demoralizing backlash. The best thing to do is to plan for it so that you are ready when it hits.

Avoid Overreacting

The switch from positive to negative coverage and commentary on an issue can take place suddenly, undermining years of effort. But you can often detect in advance the telltale signs of a coming backlash.

For example, on the surface, everybody supports the idea of helping kids with learning disabilities achieve their full potential, and federal law gives them the right to receive special instruction at public expense. But smaller school districts have balked at hiring personal facilitators for students with severe developmental problems—and in the midst of one such controversy, one district opted to pay for private schooling in a distant location, including the airfare for family visits to the student, rather than recruit and train a specialist. This strong reaction to a single challenge created controversy that could have been avoided by consulting with schools that have successfully integrated special needs students into regular classroom settings. Instead of anticipating and countering a backlash, this school district signaled that the problem was unmanageable.

Forming an Early-Warning Network

To avoid getting caught by surprise, put yourself in your adversaries' shoes and try to think as they do. This is an activity you can do on your own, but one of the most valuable functions of collaboration, such as a media working group, is to gather intelligence about themes and cases with which your opponents may attack you. By planning ahead and making the best use of your network of contacts, you will often be able to get an early warning that allows you to predict and successfully deflate the opposition.

Being Aware of Possible Media Bias

You may find that a particular media outlet, an individual reporter, or a blogger, for whatever reason, is waging a vendetta against your organization, spokespeople, or you personally. A local editor or news director may have an ideological bent or see sensational stories as a way to build audiences. A columnist or blogger with a personal bias may have an ability to turn others in the media against you.

Do not sit back and shake your head. Take action.

Always start by calling the reporter (or blogger) directly. If he or she is rude or discounts your concerns, go to the next level of decision making at the station or publication. Gather all your facts and present your case. If the editor is also uncooperative, the outlet may have an ombudsman whose job it is to examine problems brought to its attention and work with the public to find solutions. In the case of an independent blogger with no organizational ties, a possible response would be to set up your own blog just for responding to him or her, or enlisting other bloggers to help defend your organization.

Put Your Concerns in Writing

Put your objections and concerns in writing. Send a letter clearly stating what was reported incorrectly and how it should be corrected. If you have contemporaneous notes from an interview or a tape that can buttress your points, mention that in your letter and offer to supply a copy. You can ask for a retraction, correction, letter to the editor, op-ed (for newspapers), or follow-up story correcting the misinformation (or a combination of these). Ask the outlet to delete the offending story from its Web site so that the story does not perpetuate itself.

Refuse to Accept Bad Reporting

If your complaints are not resolved by the ombudsman or if no such office exists, you should move up the chain of command and speak with a top newspaper editor or a television news director. Again, put your concerns in writing and back them up with evidence. Journalists are notoriously thin skinned and may circle their wagons in the face of active criticism. But after a number of highly publicized journalism crises involving fabricated stories, editors are taking misrepresentation of facts more seriously than ever.

At some point, you need to decide if you want to fight bad coverage or "let sleeping dogs lie." Keep in mind that online searches and databases keep stories ad infinitum, and other reporters will use these as sources for other stories—unless you correct the record with follow-up stories.

If you do not get satisfaction, you may still have some recourse. If the problem occurred on television, you could request a spot or time for a rebuttal on a news or public affairs program. A television station's broadcast license comes up for periodic review by the FCC, and you can lodge a complaint at that time. Newspapers, unfortunately, have no such regulatory oversight mechanism, but you might persuade them to publish your guest editorial or letter to the editor.

Case Study: Managing Child Welfare Tragedies

Managing a child welfare agency is tricky business. All around the United States, calls about possible child abuse flood into government and private agencies, with over 86,000 cases per year opened in a state the size of Indiana. In New York City alone, 60,000 cases involving 90,000 children are investigated annually. In each case, the agency needs to determine if the abuse or neglect is serious and if a child should stay in his or her home with close monitoring or be removed from the home and placed in foster care or an institution. Many systems established and designed in the 1960s have mushroomed into large bureaucracies with shrinking budgets, and are in need of reforms. The State of Indiana and New York City have committed to major reform efforts that are tantamount to fixing a train while it is running.

John Mattingly, commissioner of New York City's Administration for Children's Services (ACS), and James Payne, director of Indiana's Department of Child Services (DCS), were recruited for their jobs by Mayor Michael Bloomberg and Governor Mitch Daniels, respectively, with the understanding that they would work to reform child welfare with a focus on safety and improving the lives of children and families.

Such reform often entails hiring additional caseworkers, encouraging retirement for burned-out social workers and managers, engaging an entire new set of community-based stakeholders, and involving a wider circle of people in placement decisions, recruitment, and standards of evaluation.

Along the road to reform, both agencies experienced terrible and tragic deaths of children at the hands of foster and birth parents. These children were either left in situations that turned dangerous or moved to one; unfortunately, a handful of cases were preventable. Had these agencies been further along in their reforms and had staff met certain expectations, things might have been different.

In most of such tragedies, media coverage is massive, with lead stories on local television, front-page headlines, blogger heydays, and seemingly endless op-eds and editorials. Legislatures, county commissioners, and city councils may also become involved in the media mix. Because of confidentiality rules, child welfare agencies are usually not able to comment on cases; however, local police, hospitals, schools, neighbors, and family members can talk (and gossip) to anyone and everyone—not a pretty picture if you are a communications director of a child welfare agency. Just as police departments cannot stop all murders, child welfare agencies, doing their very best, cannot prevent all tragedies. In the middle of a crisis, this reality is very hard to convey to the public, policymakers, and the world of children's advocates.

In a baptism by fire, Indiana DCS communications director Susan Tielking and New York City ACS communications director Sharman Stein did remarkable jobs of managing their media crises and stabilizing the situations so that reforms could continue.

Stein recalled, "My background was as a journalist. Because I had covered social welfare issues in both New York City and in Chicago, I thought I was well prepared to handle child welfare issues and any crisis that came up. When I was hired, my expectations were to be working with a handful of reporters covering the agency on a regular basis, and this was true for the first months in my job."

"But once a series of tragedies occurred over just two months, capped by the particularly high-profile murder of a seven-year-old girl who was killed by her stepfather and had been known to the child welfare agency previously, the number of reporters calling every single day skyrocketed to about twenty or twenty-five," Stein added.

The press calls, in the largest media market in the United States, went right up the media food chain and back down again. When the story broke, about ten reporters were assigned to cover the situation; in a few weeks, more than eighty reporters were working the story. In these cases, handling media coverage became a fourteen-hour-a-day job for Stein and her staff of two. The media requests actually became more difficult to handle each day. Reporters began digging for new angles while continuing to follow the obvious stories, such as funerals, grieving families, and details of the fatality. With each demand for fresh statistics, instant access to the commissioner, or the commissioner's dismissal, Stein found it difficult at first to do much more than respond. It took a few weeks before it was possible to stabilize the situation and plan ahead to begin demonstrating to the media and the public that the agency had learned from its mistakes from this case and was making substantive changes.

The challenge to stay responsive yet remain sympathetic is a big one. "Each day, we worked on our messages by showing our true compassion for the child, family members, and our workers. When a child dies in our care, the agency feels the impact of losing a child," Tielking said about Indiana. She also followed the coverage and called to correct wrong or misleading information.

Both communications directors were in the inner circle of decision making, and their executive directors were strong spokespeople who did not duck media requests, responded appropriately, ordered intensive case reviews, and took responsibility to move to action. Another important factor in their ability to move forward was that each agency had built relations with reporters, editorial boards, editors, publishers, news directors, and other media gatekeepers well before the crisis and, once coverage settled down, went back to cultivating relationships. In other cities, tragedies of this scale have led to the firing of directors and top managers, and to revolving doors of quick fixes with no lasting improvements.

The hard work of building relationships with reporters and making sure they understood the goals of the reform efforts paid off. In Indiana, the *Indianapolis Star* published a strong editorial immediately following a horrible child death, leading with "Our position: The state is making progress in protecting children from abuse. But much work remains."

The editorial went on to describe the details of the case as were known to the media, and the reforms under way, under the governor's leadership:

"The Daniels administration should take pride in its efforts to fix a child protection system that was broken for many years. . . .

"Let's celebrate the progress. It's significant. Let's also, however, remember Tajanay and . . . the many children like her still in need of protection."

This enlightened, all-important editorial in the state's leading newspaper went from the personal story and the portrait of the child, to the landscape of child welfare reform and the broader societal solutions for helping vulnerable children, paving the way for other media coverage.

Stein and Tielking agreed that crisis management and backlash prevention are "learned skills," but their most important advice is to be prepared and not to wait until the crisis hits to build a relationship with the media and public; do that from day one. You are always a phone call away from a tragedy or crisis, and the phone call usually comes from a reporter.

Watch, listen, and learn when media coverage focuses on a tragedy, disaster, or scandal. Put yourself in the position of the communications director and think how you would respond to the challenge or the phone call from a reporter that puts you or your organization in a negative spotlight. Realize that there is a light at the end of the tunnel—provided you handle the press professionally and keep grace under pressure.

Chapter 9

Selecting and Training Spokespeople

- Present a face and a name people can trust.
- Understand what is meant by "on the record," "off the record," and "on background."
- Get professional training at a price you can afford.
- Choose people carefully to represent your organization.

IT IS CRITICALLY important to choose the right spokespeople, as the messenger may be even more important than the message in establishing trust and credibility for your organization. Make every effort to limit the number of people who initiate or return press calls to one or at most two people. This may not be feasible in a large organization, but it is very important for new groups that are starting to build name recognition.

Building a name for your group and an awareness of its work may require putting one person out front even when many contribute equally to the group's success. In the nonprofit sector, and especially in volunteer groups, there may be a democratic tendency to allow anyone to speak to the press. Avoid this practice, no matter how noble the motive. If you have seven different people speaking to various media outlets, it will be harder for the public to make the connection between the individual and the group, which is something that outreach to the news media is meant to achieve.

The main public spokesperson is not necessarily a member of the communications staff. For a special project, it may make sense to recruit someone who matches the demographic profile of your target audience—for example, a young mother for an initiative affecting children, or an unemployed worker for a news conference on the need to extend unemployment benefits in a recession. As Thom Clark of the Community Media Workshop in Chicago sees it, "Often it is about having your executive director step back and put the real person with the real story in front of a camera."

And for most people, training is not just a good idea—it is a necessity. Even experienced spokespeople need some training to keep their skills finely honed.

Seeking Help from Outside: Celebrities and Third-Party Spokespeople

Seek relationships with influential people outside your organization. Enlisting a celebrity spokesperson, for example, lends instant name recognition. But there may be drawbacks: celebrities and other "high-maintenance" individuals may make serious demands on personnel or other resources, or be one paparazzo away from a personal scandal.

Identify college faculty, independent researchers, or others in your community whose work may support your agenda. They will usually be seen as fair-minded and well informed, and can help validate your work. Of course, if you have access to nationally recognized experts, by all means engage their help. But do not ignore the potential contributions of educators closer to home.

Picking the Right Spokesperson from Within

Most organizations have a chief executive, and that person is often the official spokesperson. Before you decide to confer that designation, however, make sure that the individual (1) is comfortable doing press interviews; (2) is willing to take time out of a busy schedule to deal with journalists (some of whom will ask the most annoyingly basic questions about the group's work); and (3) delivers a good presentation on television, on the radio, and in print, or is willing to be trained. This person must make the time not only to speak to the media or appear on talk shows at short notice but also to be directly involved in developing media strategies.

In a short-staffed, cash-strapped nonprofit organization, tensions can develop over how your spokesperson should spend valuable time. Is it better for the spokesperson to meet with the media, advisers, and other top policy people or to do the daily work of running the organization? If you share a clear understanding of where the media fit into your overall objectives and priorities, some of these problems can be eased from the start.

Fielding Press Calls

The person who receives a call from the media is usually not the person who will give the interview. Nevertheless, those who answer those calls should be trained in speaking to the press. When taking a message from a reporter, your staff member must determine its urgency, along with the reporter's deadline. You may have only a short window of time to reach someone who is writing a story for that night's television news or newspaper Web site—and the reporter who could not reach your spokesperson may not bother to try again.

In relaying a request for an interview to the person who will eventually grant it, there should be no more than two stops: the receptionist if you have one, and the press staffer if you have one. By establishing such a procedure for media calls, your organization will handle press calls smoothly and will give a good impression to outsiders. Reporters hate to be bounced around, never knowing if the person they are talking to has any authority to speak for your organization, and repeating their requests to a half-dozen people.

Press staff should make sure that when your spokesperson takes the call, he or she knows what the caller has been told. Likewise, the staff members should relay the nature of the request and the general thrust of the story being reported. The fewer surprises, the better the interview will go.

Speaking On and Off the Record

Popular films about investigative reporters and newsroom intrigue use the terms "on the record" and "off the record" frequently, and depict reporters and their sources as jumping on and off the record in the course of a few minutes. In fact, most media interviews are on the record, and most reporters expect them to be. Some will not even bother to conduct an interview if it is not for the record. The reason is simple enough: the reporter's main job is to gather information that can be published or broadcast. Chatting at length with someone who will not let his or her words be used can be a big waste of time, and most reporters will avoid it.

Unless you or your spokesperson has had some experience talking with reporters, you should assume that all conversations are on the record. But eventually you may need to speak on other terms. There are at least three ways of speaking with reporters:

- On-the-record interviews should be conducted only by official spokespeople. Reporters will assume that everything said to them is on the record and quotable, unless otherwise stated at the start of an interview.

- Background interviews are discussions with reporters that are held with a prior understanding that the information can be freely used in a story, but only as background, without a direct quote. Press staff should open any discussions with reporters by saying, "I would like to talk to you on background only. Most of what I will be saying will be background for publication but not for attribution. You can get direct quotes from our spokesperson." You must establish this understanding before the conversation begins, not afterward.

- Off-the-record discussions are not for quotes, not for attribution, and usually not for use in an article. Such a discussion may be useful if you need to share information with a reporter but do not want your organization quoted or identified as a source.

Sometimes an issue is so hot that nobody wants to address it on the record, yet stories containing highly sensitive information start to appear. You know you did not speak on the record, and your colleagues at other organizations had the same rule, so how did the details of that tumultuous private meeting with the governor get into the paper?

It could have found its way into print because many reporters and editors regard an off-the-record statement as fair game for reporting, as long as two or three sources confirm it. So if you choose to go off the record, understand that the substance of your conversation with a reporter could still be reported after independent corroboration. When you call to complain, he or she can simply say, "I had another source." Many experienced news sources just assume that all discussions with the press are on the record. If you do not feel comfortable making a comment, do not assume that going on background or off the record is an easy alternative.

Receiving Professional Media Training: Adding Some Polish

If you wanted to learn to play golf or tennis, you probably would not object to taking some lessons. But because speaking to the media seems simple to those who have not experienced it, many experts feel awkward attending media training sessions or reject the idea completely.

This is an error of the first order. Professional media advisers can be invaluable adjuncts to your media strategy team. They can teach you how to get your agenda across, how to construct a verbal bridge from the reporter's question to the topic you really want to address, and how to speak in complete sentences that will be quoted or used on the air. Good media coaches are very busy and highly paid. Professional fees may run upwards of $500 an hour with a half- or full-day minimum. This fee usually includes the services of a professional television camera operator using broadcast-quality equipment and a high-end playback deck.

A corporate media program may be able to afford that kind of training, but the costs may seem excessive to a smaller nonprofit on a limited budget. Fortunately, there are several low-cost options for high-return services:

- Pool the costs with other local nonprofits. Most good media trainers are willing to do small sessions with three or more participants.

- Approach the theater or communications department of a local college or university. A one-day session with a college speech or drama coach may be helpful, and it would be less costly than a session with a political or corporate media adviser.

- Try to get pro bono coaching. If your issue resonates with highly paid professionals, you might persuade them to volunteer their services "for the cause."

- Rent or purchase a videocassette player and set up a mock press interview or conference for your spokesperson. Play back the tape for immediate feedback.

- One of the best techniques for improving television performances is simple. Regularly tape your spokesperson's radio or television appearances, and organize a serious feedback session within a day or two. Several trusted advisers should be in the room to give feedback, which includes strong positive comments and gentle but firm criticism.

No matter how often reporters interview your spokespeople, there is always room for improvement. Presidents, governors, CEOs, and television anchors are always striving to improve their on-camera images. Like it or not, a spokesperson's lack of familiarity with the media can confuse or obscure your message. If your spokespeople are going to be taken seriously by the public and by policymakers, they need to make sure they are presenting messages as clearly and effectively as possible.

Doing Better Media Interviews: Quick Tips

- *Use the interview to say what you want to get across.* One way to stay on message is to prepare a message box or, as an alternative, a short list of key points on no more than one page. Keep it by your phone or workspace. If you are doing an interview over the phone, you can put the list in front of you and check off each point as you make it. Remember, you may need to make the same point several times. But when you are being interviewed in person, on radio, or on television, you'll need to do this mentally. The message box technique described in Chapter Four allows you to revisit your points without seeming rote or programmed. Moving around from the central point to the problem statement, values, and recommended action is a good way to stay on message while following the flow of a normal conversation.

- *State your messages more than once.* Think about different ways to make your main points, and try to say them aloud three or four times in the course of the interview.

- *Do not say more than you planned to say or feel comfortable saying.* Do not feel you have to fill every moment in an interview with your voice. Patches of silence will be edited out of a taped interview. For print interviews, set a time limit. When you sense that you are on the verge of saying too much, say, "I hope this has been helpful" or "Is there any more you need from me?" as you make motions to wrap up.

- *Speak in complete sentences, especially in reply to a question.* If you're asked if you think the governor is sympathetic to your latest proposal, do not just answer, "Of course," or "Hell, no." Instead say, "We think that the governor will back this idea when he sees its potential for . . ." or "We know the governor is going to be an obstacle, and we'll be ready for that when the time comes." Grunted, monosyllabic answers will not be quoted or broadcast.

- *Be memorable.* Listen to others in the media and write down the pithiest, most quotable remarks they make. Adapt them for use in your own words. Practice them aloud, even in front of your dog, so that you get used to the way they flow. Make them part of your interview agenda.

- *Do not fake it.* If you do not know the answer to a question, volunteer to get back to the caller with the information. In a live situation—on a talk show, for example—simply explain that your expertise does not extend to that area and that you do not want to make a mistake that would be repeated by others.

- *Say your organization's full name.* There is a tendency in an interview to use the full name of your organization just once at the beginning and then to refer to its acronym or some other shorthand version (such as "the center" or "the council") in later references. This is a mistake in a taped interview. The first reference may be edited out, and later ones will no longer make sense. If you embed the full name of your organization in a pithy quote, you improve the chances that the report's audience will hear it and make the right connections. You should also mention your Web site whenever possible.

- *Learn whom you will be up against.* If you have been invited to be on a talk show, assume that your worst opponents might also be invited. Find out who else has been asked, and try to do some research on that person by checking past media coverage.

- *Revise your interview as needed.* If you are in a taped-interview setting and you have started making a comment that you want to fix or revise, start from the beginning of your thought and repeat the whole thing the way you wanted it to come out. It is too much to expect that the reporter will splice a corrected ending to the good part of your first comment. Make his or her job easier and improve the chances of getting the message out correctly by taking it over from the top.

- *Be animated.* Television has a way of flattening out a personality and making a comfortable, relaxed person appear uninterested or bored. Try to do the mental equivalent of standing up straight. Keep focused, listen to each question with laser-like intensity, and then be animated and even passionate in your replies.

- *Do not play or fidget.* Television has an unblinking, unforgiving eye. Do not squirm, rock in your seat, bounce or nod at every comment, play with clothing or jewelry, or otherwise introduce any distractions into the interview or talk show.

Asking People to Tell Their Stories

Today as never before, the press tries to "put a face" on issues. Advocates of better social services to families will be asked to provide access to "real people"—families who can tell their stories. People who want more research into a cure for disease may need to bring people afflicted with that disease into the spotlight.

Anyone who hopes to engage people on the front lines of an issue has a profound ethical, moral, and sometimes legal obligation to make sure that these individuals and families are treated fairly, are prepared to talk to the press, and understand the possible implications of going public. Any group that may be called on to find interview subjects of this kind should develop internal rules and protocols for preparing families and individuals. Often, anonymity or made-up names may be necessary to protect them.

Choose Appropriate People to Tell Their Stories

Choosing the right person or family to work with the media is important, and you should consider the following:

- Work with those whose backgrounds and histories are familiar to you.

- Discuss the choice with a team of colleagues, including communications professionals or others who have experience working with media.

- Choose people who are comfortable articulating their story. If they do not feel at home talking in front of a friendly audience, do not expect them to change in front of a television camera.

Help Your Messengers by Getting to Know the Reporter

Do your homework and find out as much as you can about the reporter and the publication or broadcast outlet. Read the reporter's stories, and call colleagues who may have experience working with him or her. Meet with the reporter before the interview to ensure that there is a clear understanding about your organization or program.

Ask the reporter what type of story he or she is doing. For instance, is it a profile or an investigative piece? What is the focus, and what does the reporter expect to learn from the interview? Be sure to ask whether a photographer or cameraperson will be there, and who else will be interviewed for the story. Feel free to suggest other people whom the reporter can contact. Set parameters for the interview, including the time and location. Interviews should rarely take more than thirty minutes and almost never more than an hour.

Brief the Storytellers

Assuming that your subjects have never talked with a reporter before, your job is to explain what is being asked of them and why they were chosen. If they are beneficiaries of a service or program provided by your organization, they may not understand that they have a choice in the matter or may be reluctant to turn you down. Be certain they understand, before they ever talk to a reporter, that there will be no repercussions if they decline. Here are some things to cover:

- Tell them the purpose of the interview, and supply some information about the reporter, including his or her name and previous stories.

- Give some sense of the questions that will be asked.

- Reassure them that you will be present at all times during the interview and that you will do your best to ensure that the interview is a positive experience for everyone.

- Stress that neither they nor your organization can control what goes into the final story.

Clarify the Ground Rules for Personal Stories

Make sure the individual or family understands that they have rights, even after they have agreed to do the interview. This includes the right to stop the interview at any time if they are uncomfortable. Remind them not to talk about anything they do not want others to know. You may want to help them prepare a list of issues they want to cover, which they can share with the reporter. They have the right to decline to answer any questions they feel are too personal, and can always tell the reporter, "I'm not comfortable answering this question, but I will answer your question about . . ." Use role playing to help them practice saying no and changing the subject.

Stress that until the reporter, photographer, or cameraperson leaves the room and all the equipment is turned off, they are "on the record," and anything they say can be added to the story. Some newspapers or magazines will allow a review or check of quotes. This is not always possible, but it never hurts to ask.

Subjects do not have to agree to use their full names or photographs. If they do agree to have a photographer or television camera present, the family still does not have to agree to show their full faces. But if they do not want to show their faces, they should take precautions by putting away all family photographs (if they are being interviewed at home or at work) and any identifiable wall decorations, such as plaques and trophies. Remind the family that the reporter may have follow-up questions later on and that they, the subjects, can contact the reporter with additional information.

Discuss Best Practices for Interviews

Tell an interview subject to keep the following in mind:

- Be truthful.

- Focus on three main points throughout the interview, especially at the beginning and end.

- Tell personal stories.

- Keep it simple. Do not talk in jargon or slang or use big numbers.

- Do not speculate about what you do not know.

- Know that you are always "on the record" with a reporter.
- If you are asked questions that require a simple yes or no answer, use them as a springboard to elaborate your main points and to give real-life examples.
- Make eye contact with the reporter and the camera.
- Talk only about those things you want to see in the media.
- Never, ever lie.

Explain the Risks and Benefits

It is extremely important to let families and individuals know that there are some risks involved when doing any interview. For example, classmates at school who hear about the interview may tease the children. Parents should be asked how they feel about having coworkers, friends, or their children's teachers learn about their problems or the services they have received.

At the same time, there are definite benefits:

- Positive coverage can help build support for families and programs that serve them. A successful interview will celebrate the family's strengths and victories.
- The interview can reach those who need help.
- Personal stories can help policymakers, reporters, and the public understand people who are working to improve their own lives.

Case Study: Messengers for Expanding Early Education

In Chapter Four, we presented a case study for framing messages related to early education. We revisit the early education issue here to illustrate the importance of choosing the right messenger to speak to your target audiences.

Polling on social or community issues suggests that advocates for those issues have "standing" because of their association with the issue or cause.

However, it's important to consider expanding your messenger base to include authoritative figures outside your advocacy community. For example, advocates of expanding early care and education for children before they enter school frequently ask kindergarten teachers to attest to the links between pre-K and K–2 learning. Pediatricians may be called on to attest to the importance of early education in brain development. And a group called *Fight Crime: Invest in Kids* recruited sheriffs and prosecutors to help link early education to the prevention of criminal behavior down the road. This was particularly effective because of the unusual involvement of law enforcement personnel in childhood concerns. School nurses, family doctors, and leaders of faith-based organizations have also been credible messengers—along with businesspeople, who favor investing in early care and education because of its high "rate of return" in higher graduation rates and improved workforce readiness.

All these messenger groups were first tested in focus groups and polling surveys by the early care community.

Today pre-K is seen as part of the education reform conversation—a shift in framing that has helped secure billions of dollars in federal and state support.

Chapter 10

Capitalizing on the Power of Partnerships

- Benefit from nonprofit coalitions and media working groups.
- Enhance internal communications.
- Form media partnerships.

Collaborations and Coalitions

If partnerships are short-term efforts, they might be called collaborations. If they are ongoing or long term, they become coalitions. Working partnerships have a unique value to nonprofit communications because they amplify and reinforce your organization's work and often provide access and opportunities that would not otherwise be available.

Most nonprofit institutions are already familiar with the collaborative approach to achieving shared goals. To take this approach one step further, apply the same strategies to communications. In fact, working together on media strategies is a powerful way to coordinate a range of efforts by organizations that might otherwise compete for media attention.

Mike Pertschuk, cofounder of the Advocacy Institute and former chair of the Federal Trade Commission, tells audiences about the power of "convening potential allies for relationship building, facilitating exchange, developing strategies, and building movements." Pertschuk has dedicated a large part of his adult life to raising awareness about the health hazards of tobacco, which was one of the most successful issue-oriented strategies in the twentieth century.

He warns, however, that "at times, people's column-inch envy can become a destructive force in a coalition." Here he is referring to the internal conflict that can arise when one leader in a coalition gets more news coverage and is quoted more frequently than others. A cardinal rule to facilitating successful media efforts is to ask strategists to come to a planning meeting and to leave their egos at the door; they should put the issue above any one organization's thirst for recognition. Once people begin working together on a media message, this attitude can also help bridge some policy differences.

However, it should be recognized in a collaborative media effort that the "ask" refers to a specific policy or a set of policy directions. The importance of the collaborative process, which is needed to ensure agreement on a common set of policy directions underpinning the media strategy, cannot be underestimated. No unified integrated communications strategy can be executed without specific, detailed agreement among the collaborating organizations or individuals with regard to the policy directions embedded in the effort. Sometimes, after a great deal of staff effort, it is only possible to agree on a set of principles, rather than specific policies. This is usually enough to justify the media plan.

Increasingly, funders are recognizing that making a difference in society requires an ability to coordinate both the messages and the messengers. Funders are moving away from investments in single organizations that might carry the message and are instead focusing on implementing collaborative strategic media initiatives.

Over time, many nonprofits have found that collaboration in educational or media outreach strategies can improve their chances of funding. And by working together, groups can create a unified voice that speaks even for those who lack the resources to make themselves heard.

In a collaborative media strategy, each cooperating organization agrees that shared policy directions or policy principles are most effectively communicated by a diverse set of messengers. The case study at the end of this chapter illustrates this point.

Considerations in Establishing a Partnership

In choosing a partner in a communications program, you could consider whether the other organization has a past or continuing collaboration in some area, a positive reputation among target audiences, an ability to commit a fair share of resources, and a track record of working with others successfully. Partners could come from the business, nonprofit, or government sectors. Typical candidates for collaboration include businesses, educators, local advertising or public relations firms, police forces, social service professionals, health care professionals, religious leaders, and media representatives. In the case of the Coordinated Campaign for Learning Disabilities (CCLD), which is profiled as a case study later in this chapter, collaborating organizations included a dozen leading learning disability groups.

No matter where they come from, the partners should share a clear set of goals from the beginning. The members of the collaborative should have an opportunity to express their preferences about involvement. Then the group as a whole can agree on specific expectations and timelines for completion. Every group's contributions should be acknowledged at every step, especially at the end of the project.

Various Collaborative Models

Today's competitive media climate demands that nonprofits and public agencies consider collaborative models in order to rise above the back-and-forth of contending interests that passes for debate in the electronic age. Depending on your nonprofit's goals and your partners' wishes, you could create an ad hoc creative group responsible for coming up with the big concepts or slogans at the beginning of your initiative. Those basic ideas will need approval by the overall coalition to gain all groups' complete cooperation in employing them.

Depending on circumstances, ongoing media outreach could be then assigned either to a general advisory panel tasked with overall planning strategy and setting goals, or to a media working group that has regular meetings focused on outreach.

Media Working Group

To build a media working group on your coalition's issues, start by inviting groups that share your goals to send a representative to regular meetings, perhaps once a month, to share ideas and design specific strategies for media outreach.

- Keep the meetings to one or two hours. If possible, serve food. It improves turnout and sends a strong message that these meetings are important and worth the effort.
- Make sure the staffers responsible for communications participate.
- Make sure each meeting reviews the most recent media activities.
- Outline upcoming activities that might have a media angle.

Collaborative Research Committee

Depending on the type of strategy you adopt, you can form a research committee within the media working group by having members from each group establish goals and define the parameters of a comprehensive research project. The members can begin working together by jointly evaluating research projects, such as a media analysis or a review of existing polling data.

Informed by the evaluation of existing research, the group can select topics for its own public opinion research or focus group questions, the demographic groups to be targeted, and the discussion guide that the focus group's facilitator will use. They can attend focus group sessions as observers.

Establishing a research planning committee within the larger working group also lays the groundwork for future efforts by building internal organizational capacity and providing technical assistance on such topics as opinion research or advertising.

An Expanded Messenger Base

A media collaboration has the positive effect of expanding the number and variety of spokespeople for your agenda. It might permit you to take advantage of research being conducted on university campuses and to gain the support of business and industry leaders. Drawing on others as spokespeople for your cause can not only turn up the volume of voices but also highlight how numerous and varied they are. Assembling a pool of spokespeople with a coordinated message is a critical step in any long-term communications strategy on a major social issue.

Four groups are especially worth approaching in the early stages of a media collaboration:

- *Academic experts.* A special effort to recruit academic experts can create an informal speakers bureau to which journalists are referred for expert commentary and analysis. Note that the most credible, and approachable, academics may be those affiliated with a local institution.

- *Business leadership roundtables.* The business community is a key audience for many nonprofit and government initiatives. To reach them, link your issues to their concerns about competitiveness, productivity, and workforce development, and encourage them to think about ways to involve the private sector more in an attempt to reach your goals.

- *Faith-based organizations.* Faith-based leaders are particularly credible when expressing the needed "values" that some media efforts require.

- *Community leaders.* Community leaders can usually use their own networks to find individuals and families that exemplify the need for particular policies and can tell their story for media purposes.

Internal Communications: The Lifeblood of Partnerships

Often groups in a communications partnership initially have suspicions about working with other groups. In the media arena, news outlets compete for audiences, advertising dollars, market share, and recognition. Similarly, like-minded nonprofits may have an established pattern of competing for funding and media recognition from a limited number of charities and news outlets. In short, when considering possible partners, you should think about the likely interplay of institutional egos and even of personal ones. Good internal communications are key.

Communications Among Partners

One of the best ways to build group solidarity and cohesiveness is to make the media working group the best source of current information about your issues. Keeping the members well informed and "in the loop" has become easier with new technology. E-mail systems are excellent vehicles for regular notices, internal newsletters, or comprehensive reports between meetings. For more immediate communications, inexpensive audio briefing calls with collaborating organizations can supplement regular meetings.

A regular component of your communications strategy should be to circulate updated "message memos," which not only help coordinate your efforts but also contribute to group solidarity. If you are preparing print or broadcast materials for distribution, be sure that every partner has a chance to comment on them or to contribute to their development before they are made final. Partners should get advance copies so that they don't learn about their existence from other people.

Communications Inside Your Nonprofit

Inside your organization, staff and board members can be tremendous allies or obstacles to any communications strategy or collaboration. Staff members should have a full briefing on your communications planning process and should be encouraged to join select brainstorming sessions. From the receptionist and unpaid interns who answer the phone and greet visitors to your top management team and board of directors, everyone should receive basic training on communications skills and messages at least once a year and as part of new employee orientation. Your internal staff and board should receive all press releases and advisories, media materials, and important newspaper clippings. If it is impossible to give a copy to each staff member, then post these on bulletin boards in popular locations near mailboxes or lunchrooms.

E-mail or post on your Web site regular updates about media coverage, events, and successes. If a media crisis occurs, all staff should be given immediate notice and reminded to send all press calls to one designated person. Negative leaks from inside your organization can be devastating. If morale is low and people feel disconnected with the communications flow of your organization, internal leaks can happen. If they do, top managers will need to find ways of boosting morale and building a positive work environment before tensions boil over.

Overall, staff and board members constitute a marketing force that can help communicate your vision, values, and mission better than anyone else. Use their talents and energy wisely.

Media Partnerships

For most of the twentieth century, the press played important roles in American society both as a public conscience and as a watchdog. Journalists helped root out corruption, aid the disadvantaged, and keep public and private power in check. The muckraking tradition that began in the early part of the century helped focus public attention on slumlords and the meatpacking industry.

Several generations of investigative reporters honed and upheld that tradition, with legendary results: exposure by the *New York Times,* with the help of police officer Frank Serpico, of massive corruption in the New York City Police Department; the *Washington Post*'s unrelenting pursuit of White House involvement in the Watergate burglary and attempted cover-up, which led to the resignation of a president; and the discovery by reporters for the Gannett News Service that hundreds of deaths attributable to child abuse had gone undetected because of errors by medical examiners.

All of these stories won Pulitzer Prizes and brought prestige to their newspapers. If you have knowledge (and, more important, evidence) of official corruption, deception, or obstruction of justice, reporters can be powerful allies.

But you don't have to have a hot story to work with the news media. In the twenty-first century, media outlets are striving to become all-purpose centers of local information and opportunities for civic engagement. In fact, media partnerships with members of their communities are stronger than ever in response to shrinking audiences for news and the desire of news organizations around the country to engage people. For example,

- Local broadcast stations around the country regularly team up with nonprofits to find adoptive homes for foster children in the Wednesday's Child program.

- HBO developed a made-for-cable movie, *Iron Jawed Angels,* starring Academy Award winner Hilary Swank, about the struggle for women's suffrage. For the film's release, the cable network teamed up with many women's rights organizations during Women's History Month in March 2004 to support voter registration efforts. Each election cycle, HBO reruns the movie and taps into the same networks of voting activists; as a historical piece, the film is "evergreen."

- WGBH-TV in Boston coordinated a public outreach effort on global health called *Rx for Survival* with the Global Health Council, Save the Children, CARE, and others to mobilize communities around child survival issues in developing countries. The multipart series included partnerships with *Time* magazine, National Public Radio, the PBS Web site, and others during a year when PBS was highlighting "viewers as doers" around a host of issues and community activities.

The main criteria for success in such a project are (1) a strong commitment by all the partners, (2) public participation in the search for ways to improve news coverage, and (3) substance in the coverage that emerges. Anything less will produce a halfhearted or superficial treatment of important issues, which could further alienate news organizations and their audiences.

Broadcasts in the Public Interest

Broadcast stations are licensed by the FCC based on the principle that the media airways are a public trust, not unlike a park or a museum. The Communications Act of 1934 originally required that station licensees broadcast in "the public interest, convenience or necessity." This public interest standard was never really defined and has been translated and retranslated by the FCC, the courts, and Congress over the years. What has resulted is a greater awareness among broadcasters and cable companies of community responsibilities and the efforts of public-minded people and groups. Although broadcasters' original motivation was to meet minimum FCC requirements, today most major broadcasting companies operate public affairs programs to help build audiences and bridges to organizations that can help make them a success.

Lifetime Television Network, for example, was created in 1984 as a medical channel serving doctors and health care professionals, and featured programs on fitness, personal and family health, science, and medicine. In 1995, partly because of a change of ownership, Lifetime was revamped and became "Television for Women." Its prime-time ratings now rank fifth among all basic cable networks, just behind the major sports channels. In 1997, Lifetime was watched by almost twice as many households as CNN and three times as many as television.

A big part of Lifetime's strategy has been to build strong partnerships among nonprofit organizations around such issues as child care, breast cancer awareness, women's sports, voter registration, and women in politics. It has launched an extensive public affairs effort to keep high-quality, affordable child care a priority issue in Washington DC and around the country. Using PSAs and community outreach, Lifetime and its partners are working together to amplify the voices of women and their families and to encourage action by business and government. Lifetime has sponsored a series of events in major U.S. cities and has used its Web site to call attention to its initiatives.

Community Journalism: Reconnecting Newsrooms and the Communities They Serve

Another trend of particular interest to nonprofit communicators is the surge in projects designed to reconnect newsrooms with the communities they serve under the banner of civic or community journalism. Some journalists have been skeptical about this development, but the Radio and Television News Directors Foundation (RTNDF), which is the educational arm of the Radio-Television News Directors Association, declares, "In their efforts to remain neutral on the issues, journalists have grown detached from the concerns of their communities."

As a reasonable response to this turn of events, the RTNDF continues, "community journalism is grounded in the concept that news organizations have a responsibility not just to report on public issues, but to actively facilitate their debate and resolution. The media can and should encourage active dialogue on the issues without becoming involved in the actual decision-making." This community journalism movement sees itself as promoting "journalism at the highest level: raising issues, developing stories, and serving as a forum for debate." The key instrument for starting such a project in a given community is a partnership that can open avenues for community feedback and guide coverage of key issues by news organizations.

For example, a North Carolina partnership set out to broaden the range of election coverage to include topics that voters said were important to them during the 1996 elections, not just the topics candidates decide to emphasize. North Carolina newspapers and television stations joined forces to poll the public, and directed the subsequent coverage to include the issues they identified, along with the usual reports of candidates' sparring.

Case Study: The Coordinated Campaign for Learning Disabilities

For some time, experts have documented the impacts of undetected and unmanaged learning disabilities: school failure, low employment expectations, drug use, and a high incidence of suicide. But it was not until 1995 that public opinion research, commissioned by the Emily Hall Tremaine Foundation, documented the depth of confusion and the extent of misconceptions in the public's understanding of learning disabilities. A media analysis, eight focus groups, and a Roper Starch public opinion poll confirmed that Americans misunderstand and are confused about learning disabilities. They do not clearly distinguish learning disabilities from autism, retardation, and mental illness. Even more disturbing, this confusion is found, to some degree, among the very people to whom parents are most likely to turn when they have questions or worries about their children: teachers, school administrators, and physicians.

In response to the research initiative's findings, the Coordinated Campaign for Learning Disabilities (CCLD) was created. For the first time, the major national learning disability organizations convened as a group and joined with media and communications professionals to develop a long-term communications and public awareness strategy. CCLD's goals were defined as improving public understanding of learning disabilities and those affected and as advocating for early detection and intervention. The organizations in the coalition included the Learning Disabilities Association of America, the International Dyslexia Association, the National Center for Learning Disabilities, the Council for Learning Disabilities, the Division for Learning Disabilities of the Council for Exceptional Children, and the Parents and Educators Resource Center.

With the support of the Emily Hall Tremaine Foundation, CCLD launched a communications strategy to unify and galvanize key national learning disabilities groups into a strategies group. In its first year, CCLD established a system of regular communication among its members and built the working relationships necessary to launch a major national strategic communications initiative. Each member organization also increased its capacity for outreach by adding communications staff and technologies. A media and information kit was developed and sent to hundreds of education, health, science, and feature reporters and to key policymakers. The messages of a multiyear public awareness communications initiative were developed and refined through focus groups and other opinion research techniques. These efforts were capped by the Advertising Council's decision to produce a PSA campaign for CCLD, detailed below, under its "Commitment 2000" initiative on children and teens.

CCLD was a ten-year effort that had a formal beginning, middle, and end. Overall, it garnered free advertising and other support equal to a major, nationwide corporate campaign, making it worth a close look.

The overall communications plan included the following:

- A collaborative approach
- An emotional and positive message focused on early intervention and designed to reach select target audiences
- A corps of spokespeople to deliver the message in a consistent, compelling way
- A broad range of vehicles to deliver those messages to key target audiences: paid ads, improved internal communications capacities, and strategies to earn more and better media coverage
- Efforts to achieve sustainability through training

Collaboration in Action

All participants agreed that the best way to change attitudes and approaches to learning disabilities was to focus on young children. Identifying learning disabilities and intervening with appropriate teaching methods in the earliest grades offer the best hope for addressing problems before it is too late. Helping parents of young children recognize the signs of learning disabilities can prompt them to seek assistance from school personnel. Teachers need to be trained about identifying learning disabilities and about teaching students who have them.

To achieve these objectives and to implement the conceptual framework, CCLD undertook a comprehensive strategy around the following messages:

- Learning disabilities are common, affecting one in seven Americans.
- Individuals with learning disabilities are as intelligent as other people.
- Learning disabilities cannot be seen and may be hard to detect.
- Early intervention is critical and can sharply reduce the negative consequences of learning disabilities.

These themes and messages were developed through public opinion research and tested for effectiveness in four follow-up focus groups, and a public education and strategic communications plan was built around them. This included a paid ad in the *New York Times* in October, which is both Learning Disabilities Awareness Month and a point in the school year when parents and teachers would be likely to notice students' difficulties with reading or with other tasks that indicated a potential learning disability. Media trainings and outreach, the development of a Web site (in partnership with WETA, the PBS station serving Washington DC) and rapid response system, and fifty media events also helped win significant media coverage, including a *Newsweek* cover story.

The group also submitted a proposal to the Advertising Council, the country's preeminent public-service campaign source, for a pro bono national PSA campaign. With its acceptance as an Advertising Council client, CCLD won a first-class PSA campaign with Web banners and television, radio, and print ads urging parents to call a toll-free number or to visit the learning disabilities Web site for information. Groups also used this as a way to build membership.

Evaluation

Among the great successes of CCLD in its first full year was solidifying the strategies group and having it reach consensus on a set of clear, accurate messages about learning disabilities. It also agreed on the target audiences and made great strides in the area of media cultivation.

CCLD was encouraged by a noticeable shift in reporting about learning disabilities. Previously, coverage of this topic was limited to announcements of meetings, short pieces, or mentions in obituaries. Over several years, CCLD documented an increase in feature articles and stories explaining what learning disabilities are and what parents can do.

The Advertising Council campaign was launched in 1998 and lasted five years, with CCLD's participant organizations reporting membership increases of 35 percent, in part due to increased media coverage. Overall, CCLD's PSA campaign garnered more than $150 million in free advertising on the Web, in print, and in the electronic media.

Chapter 11

Chapters Online
Graphics, Advertising, and Evaluation

AS WE BEGAN to revise the second edition of this book, we found ourselves rewriting and revamping to address the new Internet environment. We also found ourselves one hundred pages over our allotted limit.

Rather than trim or delete useful information on graphics, advertising, and evaluation, we decided to post the full chapters on our Web site: www.ccmc.org.

Following are short overviews of each chapter. Please visit our site for these and other updated tips on strategic communications for nonprofits.

Producing Effective Graphics and Materials

In the early days of computers, predictions about a "paperless" office and society were commonplace. Since then, the amount of digital memory in use has skyrocketed, yet the use of paper still continues to increase. Whether in the form of regular mail, e-mail and Web printouts, press kits, brochures, reports, or news releases, printed matter still is part of the overall outreach strategy of effective nonprofits. Thus you should post electronic versions of key existing print publications for easy access and sharing on your Web site, and design future publications for print as well as online audiences.

Many of the basic principles of graphic design apply to print and Web, but there are guidelines for print that don't apply to the Web. And as long as people have a paper mailbox, the look and feel of printed matter can still speak volumes about your organization.

Making Paid Advertising and Public Service Announcements Work

Advertising takes a thousand forms, from skywriting and blimps to tiny labels on the fruit in the supermarket. But almost all advertising is paid communication designed to persuade or influence behavior. Advertising is a powerful force that shapes our attitudes about everything from what we eat to whom we vote for—and can be used to great effect by the nonprofit sector, under certain conditions. But every ad campaign must proceed from an understanding of both the nature of the advertising business and its relationship to the media and their audiences.

Closely related to paid advertising, but distinguished from it by the fact that they are broadcast at no cost to nonprofit organizations, are public service announcements (PSAs)—designed to promote some public good. By contrast, "earned" or "free" media result from outreach strategies to influence reporting and commentary.

Earned media are the focus of most nonprofit communications strategies, but it is useful to know something about paid advertising and PSAs; even if your plans do not currently call for them, your strategy may at some point in the future expand to include them.

Advertising is a big business, with its own language, terms, and protocols that can be daunting to outsiders. Nonprofits sometimes ignore or even disdain paid advertising in favor of PSAs and earned media coverage. That sentiment is misguided for two reasons.

First, the tools and techniques of advertising are generally adaptable to any communications strategy. Survey research, media content analysis, focus groups, and other components of a sophisticated communications strategy all started in the world of commercial marketing and advertising. Before launching a multimillion-dollar national ad campaign of any kind, you should test your themes and language on scientifically selected groups that represent potential audiences. That way, you can catch potential flaws or make refinements to your strategy before committing serious resources.

Second, paid advertising can jump-start a media outreach effort or complement it over the long term. CCMC provides detailed information about paid advertising and PSAs for nonprofits on its Web site. For an in-depth discussion of these and related issues, including cross-media communications, cost-cutting strategies, clearance challenges, and advertising experts, go to www.ccmc.org.

Evaluating Your Results

You have thought long and hard about your communications strategy, built a creative media team, followed good advice, and come up with successful approaches to get your messages across. As a result, you have secured significant favorable publicity for your collaborative in general and for your organization in particular, and you have built relationships with key journalists. But for the purposes of long-term planning and strategy, you still have one vital component to address: evaluation. What works, what does not, and why?

Impartial assessment is a prerequisite for continued improvement. It ensures accountability, facilitates coordination, points the way to next steps, and creates a record against which future activities can be judged. Setting goals and objectives in advance will help you establish benchmarks against which you can measure activities.

You need to assess *process* as well as *outcome*. The process question asks, What information and what other services are being delivered and by whom? The outcome question asks, Did we make a discernible difference? And why does that matter? Or, to put it another way, after all our activities, so what?

CCMC maintains a Web site dedicated to media evaluation. For a full discussion of evaluation tools, techniques, and special challenges—with sections on theories of change, budget, and criteria for evaluation—go to www.mediaevaluationproject.org. You will learn how to record events; measure improved institutional capacity, change in organizational participation, public opinion, and policy change; perform a media content analysis; and adapt these criteria where appropriate.

Resources

Style Manuals

Asian American Journalists Association and the South Asian Journalist Association. *All American: How to Cover Asian America.* www.aaja.org/resources/apa_handbook, 2000.

Associated Press. *The Associated Press Stylebook.* (Rev. ed.) New York: Basic Books, 2007.

Strunk, W., Jr. *The Elements of Style.* (4th ed.) New York: Longman.

University of Chicago Press. *The Chicago Manual of Style* (15th ed.) Chicago: University of Chicago Press, 2003.

Media Directories and Databases

BurrellesLuce
75 East Northfield Road
Livingston, NJ 07039
Phone: 800-631-1160 or 973-992-6600
Fax: 973-992-7675
www.burrellesluce.com

• • •

Community Media Workshop: Chicago Media Directory
2008 Getting on the Air, Online & into Print: A Guide to Chicago Area Media and Beyond
600 S. Michigan
Chicago, IL 60605
Phone: 312-344-6400
Fax: 312-344-6404
www.newstips.org

• • •

Hudson's Washington News Media Contacts Directory (Washington DC area)

Penn Hill Publications

738 Main Street, Suite 447

Waltham, MA 02451

Phone: 781-647-3200

Fax: 781-647-3214

www.hudsonsdirectory.com

• • •

Media Post

1140 Broadway, 4th Floor

New York, NY 10001

Phone: 212-204-2000

Fax: 212-204-2038

www.mediapost.com

• • •

New America Media Directory 2008 (ethnic media)

275 Ninth Street

San Francisco, CA 94103

Phone: 415-503-4170

Fax: 415-503-0970

http://news.newamericamedia.org

• • •

News Media Yellow Book

104 Fifth Avenue

New York, NY 10011

Phone: 212-627-4140

Fax: 212-645-0931

www.leadershipdirectories.com

• • •

Vocus

4296 Forbes Boulevard

Lanham, MD 20706

Phone: 301-459-2590 or 800-345-5572

Fax: 301-459-2827

www.vocus.com

Wire Services That Distribute Press Materials

AlterNet

77 Federal Street

San Francisco, CA 94107

Phone: 415-284-1420

Fax: 415-284-1414

www.alternet.org

AlterNet is an online news service for the progressive community that is visited by millions of people each month. AlterNet focuses on environmental, human rights, civil liberties, and social justice issues.

• • •

AScribe

5464 College Avenue, Suite B

Oakland, CA 94618

Phone: 510-653-9400

Fax: 510-597-3625

www.ascribe.org

The AScribe newswire transmits news releases directly into newsroom computer systems—and to the desktops of journalists—at major media organizations through the Associated Press. AScribe members' news also goes to Google News, to such news retrieval databases as LexisNexis and Factiva, and to online publications, topical Web sites, and intranets.

• • •

PR Newswire

810 Seventh Avenue, 32nd Floor

New York, NY 10019

Phone: 201-360-6700 or 800-832-5522

Fax: 212-596-1506

www.prnewswire.com

Established in 1954, PR Newswire has offices in fourteen countries and routinely sends news to outlets in 135 countries and in forty languages. Costs for distribution vary. PR Newswire distributes both national materials and state-specific information.

Media Relations for Nonprofits

There are many for-profit media organizations and public relations firms that specialize in work with nonprofits. For a list, contact info@ccmc.org.

• • •

American Forum
1071 National Press Building
Washington, DC 20045
Phone: 202-638-1431
Fax: 202-638-1434
www.mediaforum.org

American Forum has more than thirty state-based organizations that regularly distribute op-ed pieces to newspapers within those states.

• • •

Cause Communications
1836 Blake Street, #100A
Denver, CO 80202
Phone: 303-292-1524
www.causecommunications.com

Cause Communications was founded in 1997 and provides the following services: story placements in the media, media workshops, strategic communications planning, viral marketing, and Web site assistance for nonprofits.

• • •

Green Media Toolshed
1212 New York Avenue, Suite 300
Washington, DC 20005
Phone: 202-464-5350
www.greenmediatoolshed.org

Green Media Toolshed works with the environmental community to strengthen its communications infrastructure.

• • •

Mainstream Media Project
854 Ninth Street, Suite B
Arcata, CA 95521
Phone: 707-826-9111
Fax: 707-826-9112
www.mainstream-media.net

This nonprofit organization helps other nonprofits get coverage on radio stations across the country. It issues media alerts, places experts on radio programs, and coordinates its own syndicated radio show.

• • •

The National Press Club
529 Fourteenth Street, NW, 13th Floor
Washington, DC 20045
Phone: 202-662-7500
Fax: 202-662-7512
http://npc.press.org

Select cities have press clubs with facilities for news conferences and meeting rooms with reporters. For example, the National Press Club in Washington DC has excellent meeting facilities. They are a full-service venue for press conferences, forums, breakfasts, lunches, dinners, meetings, or receptions.

Their Broadcast Operations Center is a state-of-the-art, full-service digital video production facility. The Press Club offers high-quality, high-speed direct cable transmission of live video and audio from every press conference room to news bureaus everywhere, including high and low bandwidth, live or archived streaming, and webcasting of events.

For a complete list of National Press Club and Broadcast Operations Center services, go to http://press.org/facilities. Or to contact them directly, e-mail them at events@press.org or boc@press.org.

• • •

The Progressive Media Project
409 East Main Street
Madison, WI 53703
Phone: 608-257-4626
Fax: 608-257-3373
www.progressive.org

The Progressive Media Project distributes op-ed articles to newspapers across the country. Each year, two hundred to three hundred are distributed through this service. The Project also conducts writing classes for non-profits, foundations, and advocates.

• • •

Public News Service
Boulder Office
3980 Broadway, Suite 103, Box 139
Boulder, CO 80304
Phone: 303-448-9105 or 888-891-9416
Fax: 208-247-1830

Boise Office
1810 West State Street, #420
Boise, ID 83702
Phone: 888-891-9416
Fax: 208-247-1830
www.publicnewsservice.org

Public News Service is a socially responsible company that is building new models of community-accountable media. They are building a fifty-state network of cross-platform and multi-issue news services.

• • •

The Spin Project
149 Natoma Street, 2nd Floor
San Francisco, CA 94105
Phone: 415-227-4200
Fax: 415-495-4206
www.spinproject.org

The Spin Project works with a wide range of nonprofits to conduct communications audits and communications strategy development and workshops. They also host an annual Spin Academy for scores of nonprofit leaders seeking to improve their communications efforts.

Sources of Public Opinion Research

Belden Russonello & Stewart

1320 Nineteenth Street, NW, Suite 700

Washington, DC 20036

Phone: 202-822-6090

Fax: 202-822-6094

www.brspoll.com

Belden Russonello & Stewart is a national public opinion research firm that conducts polling, workshops, and message development on a wide range of progressive issues, such as civil rights, the environment, education reform, and health care. The firm's most recent reports are available on its Web site.

• • •

Charlton Research Company

Oregon Office

333 Limpy Creek Road

Grants Pass, OR 97527

Phone: 541-476-4050

Fax: 541-476-4051

Maryland Office

13017 Wisteria Drive, #452

Germantown, MD 20874

Phone: 301-515-2800

Fax: 301-515-2807

www.charltonresearch.com

Charlton Research Company publishes the *Charlton Report*, a regular assessment of public opinion. Charlton also conducts omnibus polls on national and California-specific issues. Some of the firm's polls, on a wide range of issues, are available on its Web site.

• • •

The Gallup Report Monthly
The Gallup Building
901 F Street, NW
Washington, DC 20004
Phone: 202-715-3030
Fax: 202-715-3041
www.gallup.com

The Gallup Poll has published this subscription report monthly since 1965. It contains articles from the weekly *Gallup Poll Briefing*, reprinted in full, including the poll questions, the results, and detailed demographic tables, in an easy-to-read format.

• • •

Harris Interactive
60 Corporate Woods
Rochester, NY 14623-1457
Phone: 585-272-8400 or 800-866-7655
www.harrisinteractive.com

The Harris Poll has been released several times a week since 1965. It provides up-to-date readings on the pulse of the American public by following public opinion on current issues in the news. On request, Harris Interactive will provide complete demographic details for all questions in its releases.

• • •

iPOLL Databank
The Roper Center for Public Opinion Research
Homer Babbidge Library
369 Fairfield Way, Unit 2164
Storrs, CT 06269-2164
Phone: 860-486-4440
Fax: 860-486-6308
www.ropercenter.uconn.edu/data_access/ipoll/ipoll.html

This online databank of U.S. public opinion polls is rich in subject matter. iPOLL contains nearly five hundred thousand survey questions and answers asked in the United States from the past sixty-five years by more than 150 survey organizations. iPOLL is operated by the Roper Center for Public Opinion Research and is available on the Web. A limited version of iPOLL is offered free. Yearly subscriptions and one-time searches also are available.

• • •

Lake Research Partners
1726 M Street, NW, Suite 500
Washington, DC 20036
Phone: 202-776-9066
Fax: 202-776-9074
www.lakesnellperry.com

Lake Research Partners is a national public opinion and political strategy research firm working with progressive nonprofits on such issues as women's rights, youth and children, and the environment. Polling data are available on the organization's Web site.

• • •

Pew Center for People and the Press
1615 L Street, NW, Suite 700
Washington, DC 20036
Phone: 202-419-4350
Fax: 202-419-4399
www.people-press.org

The Pew Center for People and the Press is sponsored by The Pew Charitable Trusts. The Center conducts research on attitudes toward the press, politics, and public policy issues. During election years, the Center conducts numerous polls on issues of concern to voters and the political candidates at the national level. All the surveys are available on the Center's Web site.

• • •

Public Agenda Online
New York Office
6 East Thirty-Ninth Street, 9th Floor
New York, NY 10016
Phone: 212-686-6610
Fax: 212-889-3461

Washington Office
1100 New York Avenue, NW, Suite 1090 East
Washington, DC 20005
Phone: 202-292-1020
Fax: 202-775-8885
www.publicagenda.org

Public Agenda Online was founded by prominent pollster Daniel Yankelovich. It frequently works with foundations and nonprofits to conduct survey research on such issues as education, the economy, foreign policy, the military, homelessness, and housing. All the organization's polls are available online at its Web site.

• • •

The Roper Center for Public Opinion Research
University of Connecticut
Homer Babbidge Library
369 Fairfield Way, Unit 2164
Storrs, CT 06269-2164
Phone: 860-486-4440
Fax: 860-486-6308
www.ropercenter.uconn.edu

The Roper Center for Public Opinion Research is the leading educational facility in the field of public opinion. The Center exists to promote the intelligent, responsible, and imaginative use of public opinion in addressing the problems faced by Americans and citizens of other nations. The Roper Center strives to improve the practice of survey research and the use of survey data in the United States and abroad.

Framing and Message Development

Community Media Workshop
600 S. Michigan Avenue
Chicago, IL 60605
Phone: 312-344-6400
Fax: 312-344-6404
www.newstips.org

Community Media Workshop works in the Chicago area to train individuals and organizations on how to formulate effective messages, establish good media relationships, and plan communications initiatives.

• • •

The FrameWorks Institute
1776 I Street, NW, 9th Floor
Washington, DC 20006
www.frameworksinstitute.org

The FrameWorks Institute conducts communications research to aid nonprofit organizations in expanding their constituencies, building public will, and furthering public understanding of specific social issues.

• • •

The Institute for Global Ethics
11 Main Street
P.O. Box 563
Camden, ME 04843
Phone: 207-236-6658 or 800-729-2615
Fax: 207-236-4014
www.globalethics.org

The Institute for Global Ethics works with individuals and organizations to provide publications, speakers, and other assistance to make ethics an integral part of daily life.

• • •

The Opportunity Agenda
Washington Office
1536 U Street, NW
Washington, DC 20009
Phone: 202-339-9315
Fax: 301-576-5780

New York Office
568 Broadway, Suite 302
New York, NY 10012
Phone: 212-334-5977
Fax: 212-334-2656
www.opportunityagenda.org

The Opportunity Agenda works to frame domestic policy issues while working with social justice organizations to connect messages with core American values.

Crisis Management

Harvard Business Essentials. *Crisis Management: Master the Skills to Prevent Disasters*. Boston: Harvard Business School Press, 2004.

• • •

Hennes Communications, LLC
2841 Berkshire Road
Cleveland, OH 44118
Phone: 216-321-7774
Fax: 216-321-7577
www.hennescommunications.com
www.crisiscommunications.com

Hennes Communications specializes in crisis communications, managing the media, and crisis media relations through workshops, seminars, and consultations, with a free monthly newsletter full of tips and ideas.

• • •

Institute for Crisis Management
455 S. Fourth Street, Suite 1490
Louisville, KY 40202
Phone: 502-587-0327 or 888-708-8351
Fax: 502-587-0329
www.crisisexperts.com

The Institute for Crisis Management provides crisis management services to nonprofit organizations, including crisis consulting, research, communications planning, and workshops.

• • •

Kelcom, Inc.
Kelly Burke, President
16913 Hoskinson Road
Poolesville, MD 20837
Phone: 301-407-0371
kellydburke@comcast.net

Kelly Burke is a former television newsperson with more than thirty years of experience. His firm specializes in crisis communications and television readiness training. The firm has done extensive work with nonprofits and government agencies across the country.

• • •

Schwartz, Diane. (ed.). *Crisis Management Guidebook.* New York: PR News Press, 2006.

Other Publications Worth Reading

Andresen, Katya. *Robin Hood Marketing.* San Francisco: Jossey-Bass, 2006.

Beckwith, Sandra J. *Publicity for Nonprofits.* Chicago: Kaplan, 2006.

Bray, Robert. *Spin Works!* San Francisco: Independent Media Institute, 2002.

Feinglass, Art. *The Public Relations Handbook for Nonprofits.* San Francisco: Jossey-Bass, 2005.

Fine, Allison H. *Momentum: Igniting Social Change in the Connected Age.* San Francisco: Jossey-Bass, 2006.

Goodman, Andy. *Why Bad Ads Happen to Good Causes.* Santa Monica, Calif.: Cause Communications, 2002.

Goodman, Andy. *Why Bad Presentations Happen to Good Causes.* Santa Monica, Calif.: Cause Communications, 2006.

Greenfield, James M., Ted Hart, and Michael W. Johnston. *Nonprofit Internet Strategies: Best Practices for Marketing, Communications and Fundraising.* Hoboken, N.J.: Wiley, 2005.

Holland, DK. *Branding for Nonprofits.* New York: Allworth Press, 2006.

Kirkman, Larry, and Karen Menichelli. (Eds.). *Op-Eds: A Cost-Effective Strategy for Advocacy.* Washington, DC: Benton Foundation, 2000.

Krug, Steve. *Don't Make Me Think: A Common Sense Approach to Web Usability.* (2nd ed.) Berkeley, Calif.: New Riders Press, 2005.

Lakoff, George. *Whose Freedom? The Battle over America's Most Important Idea.* New York: Farrar, Straus and Giroux, 2006.

Luntz, Frank. *Words That Work: It's Not What You Say, It's What People Hear.* New York: Luntz, 2007.

McLeish, Barry J. *Successful Marketing Strategies for Nonprofits.* Hoboken, N.J.: Wiley, 1995.

Ross, Bernard, and Clare Segal. *Breakthrough Thinking for Nonprofit Organizations.* San Francisco: Jossey-Bass, 2002.

Salzman, Jason. *Making the News: A Guide for Activists and Nonprofits.* Cambridge, Mass.: Westview Press, 2003.

Schwalbe, Will, and David Shipley. *Send: The Essential Guide to Email for Office and Home.* New York: Knopf, 2007.

Index

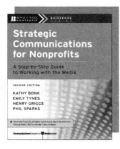

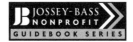